A Parish Church since Domesday
ST MARY'S, WIMBLEDON

A Parish Church since Domesday
ST MARY'S, WIMBLEDON

RICHARD MILWARD MA

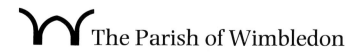
The Parish of Wimbledon

Published by
The Parish of Wimbledon
30 St Mary's Road
London SW19 7BP
1993

Designed by Sue Coley

ISBN 0 9520886 0 6

Photoset and printed in Great Britain by
BAS Printers Limited, Over Wallop, Hampshire

Contents

Main Developments

Century	At St Mary's	In the Nation
10th	FIRST CHURCH probably built	Saxon Kingdom
11th	Mentioned in Domesday Book	Norman Conquest
12th		Crusades
late 13th	SECOND CHURCH built	Edward I's Reign
14th		Black Death Hundred Years' War
15th	Building of Rectory	Wars of Roses
16th	Radical Changes inside Church	Reformation Armada
17th	Building of Cecil Chapel	Civil War Revolution of 1688
late 18th	THIRD CHURCH built	French Revolution Industrial Revolution
mid 19th	FOURTH CHURCH built	Coming of railways Victorian Empire
20th	Building of Warrior Chapel Opening of Fellowship House	World Wars Cold War

Preface

At the start of his excellent short history of St Mary's, written in 1972, Jack Harvey rightly emphasised that a parish church is not just 'a structure of architectural interest'. It is 'a living organism built by local craftsmen to minister to the spiritual needs of the people'.

The church of St Mary the Virgin, Wimbledon, has been such a centre of live Christian faith for about a thousand years. Every Sunday since before the Norman Conquest the people of Wimbledon have walked, ridden or driven from their homes to attend morning service in the Domesday, Medieval, Georgian or Fourth Parish Church. Many have been christened and married here; many have ultimately been buried in the churchyard. St Mary's is therefore the most sacred building in Wimbledon. It embodies the deepest spiritual convictions, the joys and sorrows of generation after generation.

It is true that the ultimate value of a church's work is hidden in the hearts of uncountable individuals and cannot be described in a history. Yet a history of St Mary's is essential if its undoubted influence on the local community is to be appreciated. Until the beginning of the present century it played a central part in Wimbledon life. Even today, in a so-called 'post-Christian society', its work is still important. So it is surprising that like so many parish churches it has lacked a full history – until now, the 150th anniversary of the consecration of the Fourth Church.

The writing of that history has been a real challenge for an author who is neither a parishioner of St Mary's, nor even a member of the Anglican Church. The task, however, has been made easier by the generous help of the Team Rector, Canon Gerald Parrott, his Curate, the Revd Andrew Studdert-Kennedy, Dr Thomas Cocke (Secretary of the Council for the Care of Churches), Dr David Robinson (County Archivist, Surrey Record Office), Dudley Buchanan, David Heaton, Alan Kimber and my brother John Milward. All kindly read the entire text and made many valuable suggestions. The final chapters would still have been difficult to write without the help of five senior parishioners: George James, Tony Loveband, Rosamond Tosh, Richard Walliker and Derek Witts. They willingly talked about their memories of St Mary's and then read the text to check its accuracy. In addition, an invaluable account of services at the church under

Canon Haygarth was provided by Mrs Morrell who recently celebrated her 100th birthday.

Many others have helped in the production of this book, especially:

John Craig at Fellowship House, who gave me considerable assistance with modern parish records;

The Archivists at Lambeth Palace Library and the Surrey Record Office who allowed me to search their records and use photographs of documents in their collections;

The Wimbledon Society which gave permission for the use of many of the illustrations from their fine collection; its Chairman, Norman Plastow, who photographed a number of these illustrations himself; and Arthur Whitehead who allowed me to use the drawings of the Medieval, Georgian and Victorian churches from his little booklet, *The Bells of St Mary's*.

Margaret Young who arranged for new photographs of the church to be taken by Russells and the Raynes Park Camera Club; Mary Warre who kindly shared her researches into the Faculties granted St Mary's; Tony Winship who willingly climbed a ladder to find details of a window blacked out by the crib.

John Wallace who has drawn the fine maps and plans for the book.

And Sue Coley who has gone to great trouble in typing the text, arranging its layout and preparing the book for the press.

I dedicate this history to the priests and parishioners of St Mary's, past, present – and future.

Richard Milward
January 1993

The plaque commemorating the consecration of the church. It was originally on an outer wall; it is now hidden in a Vestry cupboard.

THIS CHURCH WAS ENLARGED AND CONSECRATED MARCH 20TH 1843 — DAN^L WITHEM — THO^S DAVIES — CHURCHWARDENS

20 March 1843

Consecration of the new St Mary's

In the spring of 1843 Charles Greville, Clerk to the Privy Council, wrote in his Diary: 'The political world is all out of joint. Peel [the Prime Minister] is becoming very unpopular. Ireland is in a flame. The whole country is full of distress, disquiet and alarm. Religious feuds are rife. The Church and the Puseyites are at logger-heads. Everybody says it is all very alarming and God alone knows what will happen, and everybody goes on just the same, and nobody cares except those who can't get bread to eat.'

On Monday 20 March *The Times* was not in such an apocalyptic mood. Its tightly packed columns had little real news for its readers. The French had made 'a new conquest' in the Pacific – Tahiti. In China another island, Hong Kong, had just been ceded to 'Her Britannic Majesty in perpetuity'. There had also been an earthquake in Lancashire and Cheshire.

That Monday William Howley, the aged Archbishop of Canterbury (who had crowned Victoria Queen only five years before), had agreed to consecrate the rebuilt parish church of St Mary the Virgin at Wimbledon. He could have used the recently opened London and Southampton railway, whose terminus at Nine Elms was only a few hundred yards to the south of Lambeth Palace. But Howley, 'the last Archbishop of Canterbury to live like a Prince of the Church', preferred to travel in state. So, accompanied by outriders, he was driven in his carriage

Archbishop Howley at the coronation of Queen Victoria in Westminster Abbey. He is standing in front of the altar in a dark cope.

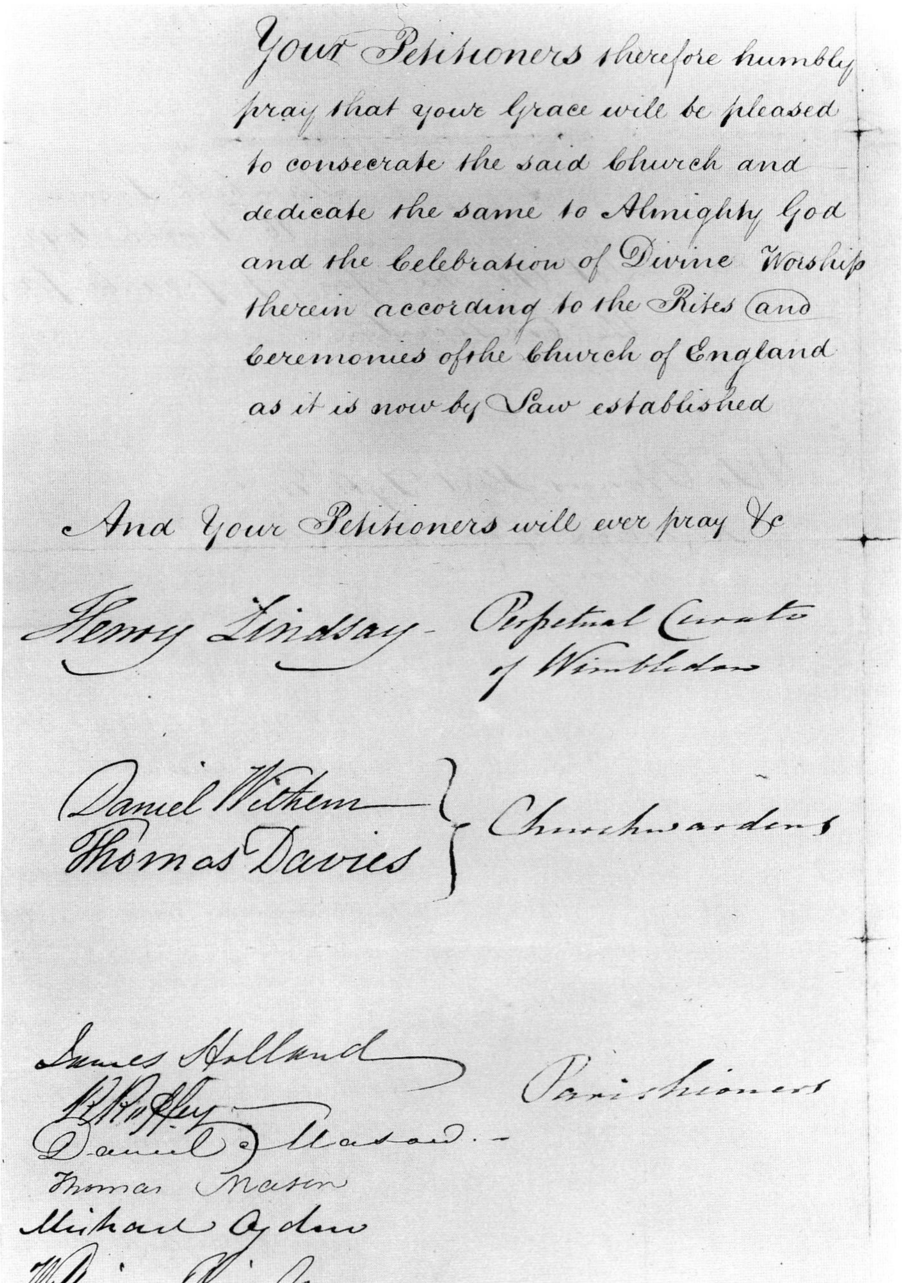

*Your Petitioners therefore humbly
pray that your Grace will be pleased
to consecrate the said Church and
dedicate the same to Almighty God
and the Celebration of Divine Worship
therein according to the Rites and
Ceremonies of the Church of England
as it is now by Law established*

And Your Petitioners will ever pray &c

Henry Lindsay — Perpetual Curate
of Wimbledon

Daniel Withers
Thomas Davies — Churchwardens

James Holland
R. Rogley
Daniel Masard —
Thomas Mason
Michael Ayden
William Kinock — Parishioners

The conclusion of 'the Humble Petition of the Perpetual Curate, Churchwardens and
Parishioners of Wimbledon' to the Archbishop for the consecration of St Mary's.

Henry Lindsay (1790-1859),
Vicar of Wimbledon 1819-1846.
He then became Rector of
Sundridge in Kent.

the few miles along the Portsmouth Road to the gates into Earl Spencer's Wimbledon Park. There he saw for the first time Gilbert Scott's impressive tower and shingled spire two hundred feet high.

At the church door he was welcomed by the Vicar, the Revd Henry Lindsay, his Curate (who had in fact been looking after the parish since 1830) Revd William Edelman, the two Churchwardens, Daniel Withem and Thomas Davies, and the Parish Clerk, John Bishop. Inside the church under the fine hammer-beam roof he went in procession up the aisle to the vestry. He passed between new pews occupied by the respectable High Street shopkeepers, such as the grocer Thomas Mason, the butcher Michael Ogden and the tailor Richard Roffey. Looking down on him from their seats in the galleries over the side aisles were the wealthier parishioners, important men like the Earl of Cottenham, Lord Chancellor at the time of the Queen's accession, and Justice Park, a leading judge who lived at Merton Grove. On either side of the new organ sat two of the most important families, the Peaches of Belvedere House who had presented the organ and the Marryats of Wimbledon House, Parkside, who had given the Royal Coat of Arms over the chancel arch.

From the vestry the Archbishop processed into the oldest part of the church, the medieval chancel which had not been affected by the rebuilding. It still had two big pews for the family at the manor house (in 1843 the Duke and Duchess of Somerset who had leased it from Earl Spencer) and at the east end the communion table with a painted board above it, on which were inscribed the Ten Commandments. A chair had been placed by the communion table and the Archbishop sat there to listen to the 'humble petition' of the Vicar asking him to dedicate the church 'to Almighty God and the celebration of Divine Worship according to the rites of the Church of England'. His response was first to make another procession round the church saying the twenty-fourth psalm and then to return to the chancel for a series of prayers, followed by the 'sentence of consecration':

'We, William by Divine Providence, Archbishop of Canterbury, by virtue of our power set apart the church and ground on which it is erected from all unhallowed uses and do dedicate it to Almighty God and Divine Worship, and decree that it ought to remain consecrated for ever.'

The Vicar then read 'the Service of the Day'. The Archbishop took over for the Service of Holy Communion, but asked Lindsay to preach the sermon. The ceremony came to an end at about mid-day with the blessing and everyone adjourned to the Dog and Fox in the High Street for 'refreshments'. Exactly what these consisted of is not recorded, but the bill came to just over seventeen pounds (five hundred pounds in modern terms), so a great deal was obviously eaten and drunk.

The Evidence

Surprisingly few records of the Archbishop's visit have survived. The only account of the consecration of Gilbert Scott's church appears to be the Order of Service for 20 March which can be found among the archives at Lambeth Palace Library. *The Times* completely ignored the event, while there was as yet no local paper to describe it in detail. Even the minutes of the Vestry meeting simply mention that the consecration took place.

This sad lack of evidence is true of a great deal of the history of St Mary's. It is therefore not possible to provide a continuous account of the church's origin or of its development during the Middle Ages. From the period of the Reformation more documents survive, but it is only from the middle of the eighteenth century that a real history can be written – and since the 1850s there is almost too much information.

PART ONE

The Domesday Church

Wimbledon and Canterbury

It was Archbishop Howley who reconsecrated St Mary's in 1843 because 'from time beyond memory' Wimbledon had been part of the Diocese of Canterbury. Geographically the village should have been in the Diocese of Winchester, but from perhaps as early as the seventh century until Henry VIII's Reformation in the sixteenth it had been part of a manor belonging to the Archbishop of Canterbury. So along with his neighbouring manors of Croydon, Cheam and Waddon, the parish formed a special area known as a peculiar. Its priests were chosen by the Archbishop; its church laws were enforced in the Archbishop's Court of Arches; and its church buildings were inspected on behalf of the Archbishop by the chief administrator of the peculiar, the Dean of Croydon.

The link with Croydon is significant. When Saxon England was officially converted to Christianity in the seventh century, the earliest churches were known as minsters. They were centres for itinerant priests who went round the neighbouring villages converting the ordinary people and saying Mass in the open air by the side of specially blessed stone crosses. Croydon was one of the early minsters in Surrey and Wimbledon was almost certainly one of the villages served by the priests.

After the Viking invasions of the ninth century, however, minsters declined in importance. Instead lords of the manor like the Archbishop of Canterbury built churches in the chief villages and appointed priests to serve them. So by the tenth century when England was reunited under the House of Wessex (some of whose kings were crowned at Kingston), Wimbledon probably had a church of its own.

'There is a church'

The first evidence that this church certainly existed is to be found in the Domesday Survey prepared in 1086, twenty years after the Norman Conquest. It did not mention Wimbledon by name but the entry for the Archbishop's manor of Mortlake, which also included the

WIMBLEDON'S FOUR DIOCESES	
7th Century to 1846	Canterbury
1846 to 1878	London
1878 to 1905	Rochester
1905 to today	Southwark

13

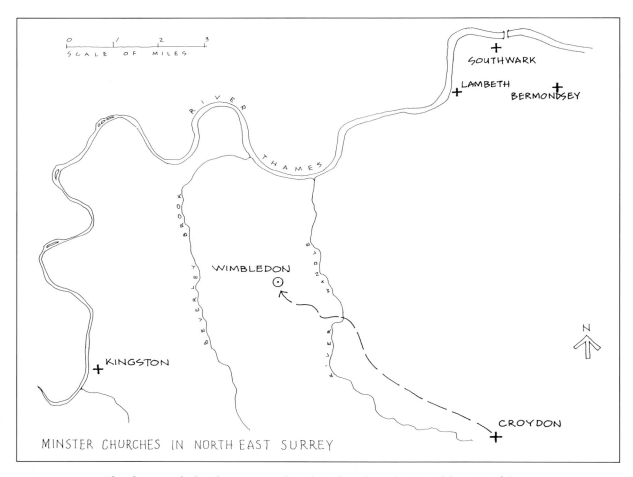

MINSTER CHURCHES IN NORTH EAST SURREY

The places marked with a cross are thought to have been the sites of the original Saxon
churches in the area. Their clergy served the neighbouring villages (e.g., Wimbledon
from Croydon).

villages of Putney, Barnes and Wimbledon, declares: 'There is a church . . . [in
the manor]'.

That church can only have been at Wimbledon. Until the twelfth century
Mortlake, Putney and Barnes do not seem to have had even chapels of their own
and for a further five centuries their 'chapelries' remained dependent on
Wimbledon. The reason for the choice of Wimbledon as the 'mother church' of
the manor is a mystery. The manor house, which often influenced the site of

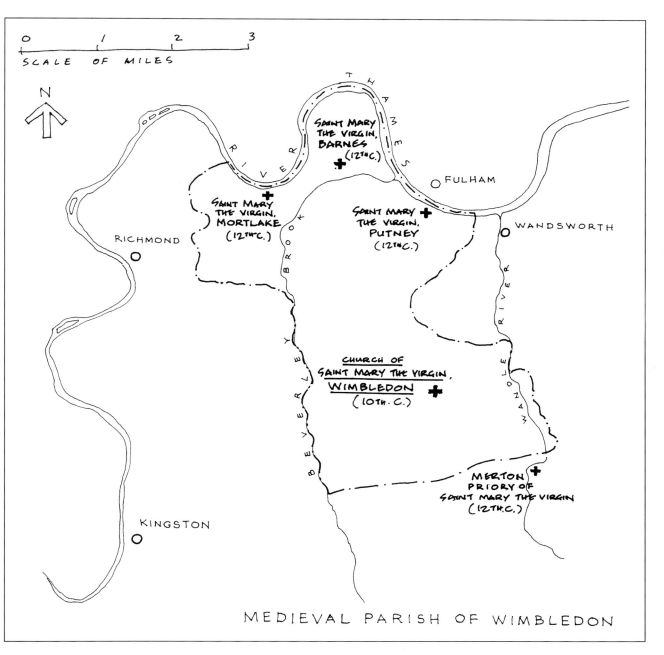

The parish extended from the boundary of Merton to the Thames. It included all the villages in the Domesday manor of Mortlake.

the church, was at Mortlake, yet its inhabitants along with those from Barnes and Putney had to walk several miles across the Common to Wimbledon every Sunday. Wimbledon may have been chosen because its church on a height would be visible from some distance. More likely its old links with Croydon helped.

The First St Mary's

The church mentioned in Domesday was almost certainly on the site of the present building. No trace of it has ever been found, but the height and dimensions of its medieval successor (probably built on its foundations) suggest it was relatively large for the period and made of masonry or wood, with a steep roof. It would have consisted of a nave where the congregation from the four villages of the manor stood packed together on an earth floor covered with straw or rushes, and a tiny chancel where the priest conducted the services from a small altar. It would only have had a few narrow windows without any glass in them. So the church was dark and draughty.

The main service would have been the Mass in Latin. Few in the congregation would have understood the words, but all were near the altar and could at least hear the priest. There was no pulpit, so if there was a sermon it would have been preached from the altar. The parishioners also came to church for baptisms, marriages and funerals. The largest building in the village, it was the focus for the most important events in their lives.

Around the church was the graveyard. The dead were buried in shrouds, not coffins and there was nothing to mark the grave, except a small mound. So the churchyard formed an open space ideal for festivities. In addition, from Norman times it was used systematically. Burials started by one wall and went across to the opposite wall, then began again over the first graves. Any bones found were placed in a small crypt under the church known as a charnel house. So, as one historian has written, 'the living at prayer were perched upon a thick platform of the dead awaiting resurrection'.

PART TWO

The Medieval Church

'ECCLESIA DE WYMBELDON'

Dedication to St Mary the Virgin

For the past two hundred years the parish church has generally been known as the church of St Mary the Virgin. In the Middle Ages, however, it was always referred to as the 'ecclesia de Wymbeldon'. Nonetheless, the dedication to the Virgin was probably given by one of the Archbishops long before its first mention in an eighteenth century document. Under the Norman kings there was a great increase in devotion to Mary and all over England churches were dedicated in her honour. Wimbledon's three daughter churches, at Mortlake, Barnes and Putney, were all named St Mary's, while the large Priory at Merton was dedicated 'to the honour of the Most Blessed Mother of God and Ever Virgin Mary'.

At such churches the Patronal feast was celebrated in a particularly solemn way. (In the Middle Ages, the feast of Mary's Assumption into heaven, 15 August, was often chosen rather than her Visitation or Nativity, as today.) Inside the church a statue of the Virgin would be placed in a prominent position, often in its own Lady Chapel at the top of a side aisle.

Whether Wimbledon had a special feast day or a Lady Chapel is unknown as the medieval records of the church are very poor. But it would be strange if the village had neither or if the people showed less devotion to their patron saint than those elsewhere. That devotion would have been especially fervent during the terrible outbreaks of plague in the century after 1348, followed by the lawless period of the Wars of the Roses, only ended by the victory of Henry VII in 1485.

The Second St Mary's

At some time during the Middle Ages, probably in the reign of Edward I (the late thirteenth century), the church was rebuilt, this time certainly in stone, but retaining as much as possible of the old nave. The chancel was extended eastwards to its present size. The medieval masonry is still the basic fabric of the present walls. At the same time a large screen was put up across the chancel

17

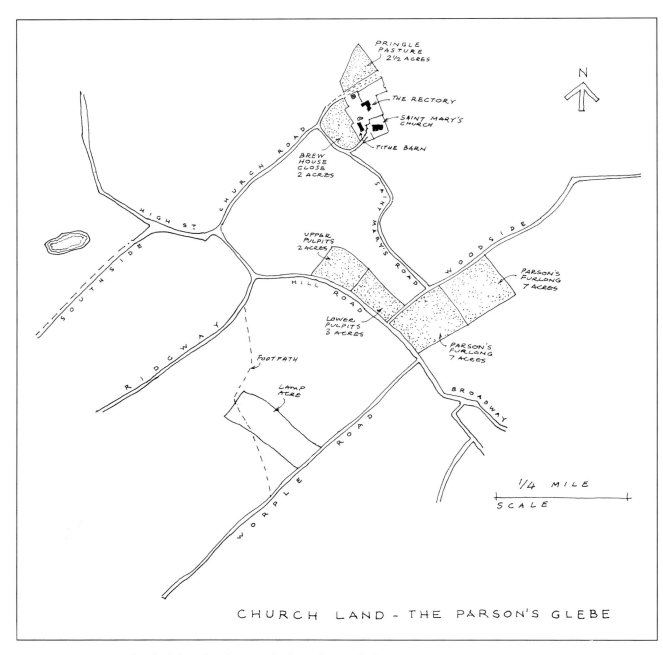

PRINGLE
PASTURE
2½ ACRES

THE RECTORY

SAINT MARY'S
CHURCH

TITHE BARN

BREW
HOUSE
CLOSE
2 ACRES

CHURCH ROAD

HIGH ST

SOUTHSIDE

RIDGWAY

SAINT MARYS ROAD

UPPER
PULPITS
2 ACRES

HILL ROAD

LOWER
PULPITS
3 ACRES

WOODSIDE

PARSON'S
FURLONG
7 ACRES

PARSON'S
FURLONG
7 ACRES

FOOTPATH

LAMP
ACRE

BROADWAY

WORPLE ROAD

N

¼ MILE
SCALE

CHURCH LAND - THE PARSON'S GLEBE

The shaded land to the east of Hill Road was called, appropriately, Parson's Furlong and
Pulpits. It formed part of one of the large arable fields. The land near the church was
for pasturing the Parson's cows, sheep and horses. Lamp Acre provided money for a lamp
kept burning in the parish church.

arch, supporting the rood or crucifix, in front of which burnt a lamp whose supply of oil was ensured 'in perpetuity' by a gift of land (including 'one acre in Westfield called Lamp Acre', about where St John's Church is today). Further changes were made in the fifteenth century when new windows were installed in the latest Perpendicular style, full of stained glass. Those on the north side of the chancel showing St John the Baptist, St Christopher and St George survived until the 1780s. Now only St George is left, transferred to the Cecil Chapel.

In the nave the congregation had more room – which they needed because the population had probably doubled since the Conquest, though after 1348 it fell dramatically. With Mortlake, Barnes and Putney building their own chapels by 1300, only the people of Wimbledon now came to St Mary's. They entered through a new south porch into a south aisle built to provide room for another 'awlter', probably in honour of St Mary. They were summoned to church by three bells ringing from a wooden bell turret crowned by a small spire above the west end of the church.

This engraving of the medieval Church was published in 1796, eight years after the nave had been pulled down. It shows a surprisingly high roof with the wooden bell tower above it, some very irregular windows, the main entrance at the west end, a south porch with the date 1637 above it, the Cecil Chapel on its right and a few graves in the churchyard.

Yet the only known pictures of the medieval church (two from its last years in the late eighteenth century) do not look very impressive. They show a very ordinary building, not to be compared to any of the great parish churches that were then going up all over England. They suggest that after building the original Domesday church, the Archbishop was less concerned with Wimbledon which he rarely visited, than with Mortlake, the site of his manor house. And in medieval Wimbledon there were no other wealthy inhabitants willing to finance a fine new Perpendicular church.

Nonetheless, the services in the medieval St Mary's must have looked impressive. The walls would have been covered with religious paintings; there was stained glass in every window; on the rood statues shone brightly in the light of the candles. The altar had a silk frontal, while the priest's vestments were

---

A LEPER WINDOW AT ST MARY'S?

In 1919 during the building of the Warrior Chapel a low side window was revealed in the chancel. It came to light when a corner fireplace in the old vestry was removed. There was no groove for glass and the presence of a vertical iron bar suggested it had probably been closed with a shutter. It seemed to date from the rebuilding of the chancel in the late thirteenth century, at a time when the floor of the church was nearly two feet lower than it is today. But its purpose was uncertain.

It has since become known as 'the Leper Window'. According to one book on the church it was possibly used 'to administer the sacrament to diseased people forced to remain outside'. Another booklet claimed that it was meant 'for those suffering from the plague to witness the consecration of the sacrament'. Even more extraordinary uses have been suggested – 'for lights to scare away demons from graves' or for a special grille through which Franciscan friars could hear confessions.

Experts, however, dismiss all these theories. They say it is a 'lynchnoscope', a low westernmost window on the south side of the chancel. In churches built before 1350 such unglazed, but shuttered windows were common. Their use was to provide ventilation from the smell of burning incense or from the heat and smoke generated when many candles were alight during important ceremonies. It has also been suggested that one purpose was to allow the parish clerk during the week-day Mass to ring a 'sacring bell' above the chancel. This was done so that, according to Archbishop Peckham writing in 1281, 'at the elevation of the Body of Christ the people who had not the leisure daily to be present at Mass may bow their knees'.

The low side window of the medieval chancel. This photograph was taken shortly after it was found in 1919 while the Warrior Chapel was being built.

The window as it is now displayed in the Warrior Chapel. The plaques round it commemorate men from Wimbledon killed in the two World Wars.

of silk, satin or damask. By 1500 there was also a pulpit in the church and the first pews for richer members of the congregation. But there is no sign of an organ or mention of a choir.

Many of these changes could only have been carried out with the active help of the laity. While the priest was responsible for the chancel, they took over the maintenance and repair of the nave, along with the provision of books, vestments and candles for the services. From the thirteenth century this work was controlled by two Churchwardens, one appointed by the parish priest, the other elected by the parishioners. They raised the necessary money by festivities such as church ales, as well as by gifts from generous members of the congregation. Sadly, not one of the names of Wimbledon's medieval Churchwardens has been recorded. Yet their work was vital for the church.

The Parish Priests

The parsons who were advised by these Churchwardens would not normally have been the official priest or Rector. These Rectors were appointed by the Archbishop of Canterbury (or on a few occasions by the King or even the Pope) and were often ambitious young clerics. They had no intention of residing in the parish and used St Mary's simply as one of their sources of income. That income was considerable: in 1291 £20 a year, by 1428 £40, about four times the average for a parish priest. It came mainly from 'the glebe' – land in the open fields, including several acres to the east of Hill Road, known later as 'the Parson's Furlong' (where the Public Library is today) and 'Pool Pits' or 'Pulpits' (on the site of modern Leeward Gardens), and from 'tithe' – a tenth of all the villagers' produce (including corn, hay, wood, wool, animals, geese and eggs), which was stored in a large barn just to the west of the church. In addition, there were the Easter offerings from the congregation, as well as fees for conducting baptisms, marriages and funerals.

Consequently, St Mary's numbered among its medieval Rectors some very distinguished priests. Among them were two Italian Cardinals, two Royal Chaplains, a future Head of an Oxford College, a Chancellor of Chichester Cathedral, and two Lord Chancellors, one the Bishop of Winchester, and the other the Archbishop of Canterbury. (This Rector, Walter Reynolds, has been described as 'intellectually and morally of all medieval Archbishops the least deserving of respect'. Yet in 1925 a fine bronze tablet in his honour was unveiled in the chancel by a far more distinguished successor, Randall Davidson.)

MEDIEVAL RECTORS AT ST MARY'S

This list is based on the researches of Alfred Arber Cooke (author of *Old Wimbledon*, 1927). It amends the list made in 1929 by A.W. Hughes Clarke for the plaque in the church.

c 1210	Philip	
c 1235	Peter de Aquablanca	Physician to Queen Eleanor of Provence, wife of Henry III
1290	John de Ausone	Chaplain to Queen Eleanor of Castile, wife of Edward I
1298	Walter Reynolds	Bishop of Worcester; Lord Treasurer; Lord Chancellor; Archbishop of Canterbury
1309	Hugh de Derby	
1310	John de Sandale	Chancellor of Exchequer; Lord Chancellor; Bishop of Winchester
1316	Walter de Kemesy	
1317	Adam de Murimoth	Canon of Hereford; Precentor of Exeter
1326	Bertrand de Monte Faventio	Italian Cardinal
1342	Adam de Newbald	
1348	Adomar	Italian Cardinal
1351	William de Cheston	Chaplain to Queen Philippa, wife of Edward III
1356	Richard Claymond	
1361	Bretel Avenall	
1361	Walter Dawtrey	
1362	John de Kennington	
1365	William de Beverley	Prebendary of St Paul's
1369	Adam Holme	Probably resident
1399	John Blackwell	Probably resident
1430	Thomas Astley	
1433	William Lindwood	
1434	Stephen Wilton	Doctor of Common Law
c 1448	Henry Severe	Great Almoner to Henry VI; Warden of Merton College, Oxford
1471	Edmund Lichfield	Chancellor of Chichester Cathedral
1474	Thomas Wilkinson	
1476	John Jevan	Fellow of All Souls College, Oxford
c 1500	Thomas Green	Bachelor of Canon Law. Probably resident
1507	Robert Wicks	Resident
c 1522	Thomas Mylling	Resident
1540	John Browne	Canon of Windsor

The Rectory from the churchyard. (*opposite*) The bronze tablet to Archbishop Walter Reynolds, unveiled in the chancel in 1925.

With the Rector often an absentee, the work of caring for the spiritual needs of the parishioners was left in the hands of a poorly-paid Vicar (or 'vicarius', a substitute). The names of very few early Wimbledon Vicars have survived: John de Grafton in 1310, Adam Sleddale in 1362 and Robert Stoughton in 1467. Two of the later resident Rectors also had Curates (assistants to his 'cure' of the parish): John Hertylpole in 1505 and John Salcock in 1540. They would probably have been of humble birth, but had to be of 'good character' with 'a simple understanding of the faith'.

How effective they were in explaining that faith to their parishioners will never be known. But at least two local men, Adam and John 'called Payn', were ordained to the priesthood in 1286, probably in St Mary's, by Archbishop John Peckham. A hundred years later another cleric, Richard Wimbledon, whose ancestors at least must have been local, was a famous preacher.

In the last thirty years before Henry VIII's Reformation the Rectors began to reside in the parish again. They were almost certainly attracted by the palatial new Rectory built about 1500 just to the north of the church by Cardinal Morton, Henry VII's Archbishop of Canterbury. All were well connected and well educated. The first was Thomas Green, a Bachelor of Law, who died in 1507 and left in his will money for the repair of the church and for one of the new printed missals for use in the services. His successor, Robert Wicks, was the son of a leading lawyer and brother-in-law of Cardinal Wolsey's secretary, Thomas Cromwell. When he died about 1522, Thomas Mylling became Rector. He may have been related to a contemporary Bishop of Hereford of the same name; he was certainly very friendly with the Bishop of London, Edward Bonner. His will (where he describes himself as 'clerk of Wymbleton') shows that he lived very comfortably at the Rectory. He had eight servants to look after him and his guests, as well as a Curate and a chaplain to help with his spiritual duties. He was also in the habit of travelling to Canterbury as he left the large sum of ten pounds 'to amending the highway between Canterbury and Chatham'. Like his parishioners he can have had little idea of the crisis that was soon to transform the Church.

Walter Reynolds
Rector of Wimbledon 1298 Canon of St Pauls
Bishop of Worcester 1308 Lord Chancellor
Archbishop of Canterbury 1313

THE FIRST PARISH REGISTER

It is a large parchment book of 150 pages, headed: 'Register of Baptisms, Marriages and Marriages and Burials in the reign of Henry VIII. From AD 1538'. In fact, up to 1594 only baptisms were recorded. The book, 'which did cost seven shillings and three pence', was not bought until 1599, so all entries for the first sixty years had to be carefully copied from an original paper register, with each page signed by the 'chyrchwarddenes, Wm. Ball and Jhoseph Wyght'. Until the 1660s the entries look as if they were all written up at the end of each year by successive Churchwardens. After the Restoration, however, the Vicar took over.

   The first Register continued in use until 1679. In the next 133 years it was followed by seven further volumes. They are now kept at the Surrey Record Office. A printed version of all the registers was made in 1924 by A.W. Hughes Clarke.

ST MARY'S DURING THE REFORMATION

First changes under Henry VIII

Thomas Mylling died on 3 November 1540 and was buried in front of the high altar at St Mary's. Over his grave a brass was fixed with a Latin inscription asking those 'who pass here to pray that his soul may reign with those above.' In his will Mylling had commended himself 'to Almighty God, our Blessed Lady St Mary the most holy Virgin, and all the company of the Blessed Saints in heaven'. Within twenty years such prayers for the dead were to be strongly discouraged.

   In the decade before his death, Mylling would have had plenty of warning that radical changes were coming in the church. In 1533 as the King prepared to defy the Pope and marry Anne Boleyn, the elderly Vicar of Isleworth, John Haile, was overheard denouncing the marriage as 'the undoing of England' and 'a sufficient cause of rebellion'. He was arrested, found guilty of treason and hung at Tyburn. A year later, along with other parish priests, Mylling was summoned to Lambeth Palace and told to swear obedience to Henry as Supreme Head of the Church in England. Like all his colleagues, he duly took the oath; his clear signature can be seen on a document in the Public Record Office. In addition, he was required to explain the change in allegiance to his congregation and regularly denounce 'the pretended power of the Bishop of Rome'.

   The changes did not stop at questions of authority which probably made little difference either to the Rector or to his congregation. Far more disturbing were the Injunctions from Thomas Cromwell, the King's Vicar-General in religious affairs and a Protestant sympathiser. With his fellow priests, Mylling was told to lay far less stress on the need for confession and on devotion to the Saints, above all to the parish patron, the Virgin Mary. He also had to buy a copy of the *Great Bible*, a new English translation made by a Reformer, Miles Coverdale, and place it on a stand in the parish church so that all could read it. Next, he learnt that control of the Wimbledon manor and of its church had passed from the Archbishop of Canterbury to the King. Finally, in April 1539 he would have heard of the take-over by the King's agents of Merton Priory, one of the larger monasteries in Southern England, and of the quick demolition of its fine church to be used as hard-core for Henry's Nonsuch Palace which was being built at Cheam.

Yet on the surface the religious life of the parish was unchanged. Mylling continued to say Mass in Latin and to preside at the processions and other festivals at the church. He carried out baptisms, marriages and funerals as in the past, though he now had to enter details in a new Parish Register which by law he had to keep. His first entry was on 13 January 1539: the baptism of Elizabeth Wight. Despite this air of normality, he clearly feared that worse was to come. He was a wealthy man, but when he came to make his will, he left his money

The first entries in the 'register booke of the names of all such persons as have bene christened in ye parish of Wimbledone in the county of Surrye since the thirteene day of January in ye thirty yeere of the raigne of our soveraigne Lord Kinge Henry the eyght anno 1538'. Then follow the names of Elizabeth Wight, Thomas Simpson and Ann Jux.

to his relatives, friends, servants – and for road repairs. There was nothing for St Mary's.

Significantly, his successor was one of Henry's chaplains, John Browne. As both an MA and a Bachelor of Theology, he appears too learned for most of his parishioners. Moreover, he no longer had an incentive to live at Wimbledon as the king had now taken over the Rectory – and in December 1546 stayed there for two nights while travelling slowly back to Whitehall seriously ill. At the same time in return for some land, Henry transferred control of the church to the Dean and Chapter of Worcester Cathedral, who from now on became Rectors of Wimbledon. The parish priest was demoted to Vicar or more exactly to Perpetual Curate (which meant that he could not be dismissed by the Rectors, but was only paid a small annual stipend). Browne was allowed to keep the courtesy title of Rector until he left Wimbledon in 1554, but he had to accept an immediate drop in income from about £80 a year, mainly from the valuable tithes, to a salary of £13.6s.8d., paid out of the tithes with the rest all going to William Cecil who in 1550 leased the Rectory from the Dean of Worcester.

Transformation under Edward VI and Elizabeth I

John Browne and his successors had to face far more unsettling changes in the years after Henry VIII's death. Under the young Edward VI (1547-53) and then his half-sister Elizabeth I (1558 – 1603) the Reformers became dominant. They set out to cleanse the church of what they felt were 'Popish superstitions'. They

---

THE FIRST VICARS

1555	Thomas Young	
1562*	William Hartford	
1570s, 80s	No record of any Vicar	
1590*	Meredith Price	
1601	Robert Townson MA	Dean of Westminster; Bishop of Salisbury
1605	Daniel Mead	
1617	Richard Edwards	
1624*	Anthony Evat	
1630	Christopher Fox MA	

*Extra names found since the list in the church was made

A tapestry picture hung in the Vestry of Thomas Cranmer, the last Archbishop of Canterbury to own the Manor of Wimbledon. He is shown being burnt at the stake (most unhistorically with Bishops Ridley and Latimer).

insisted that services should be in English, not Latin, and based on Protestant texts rather than the Roman Missal. They therefore produced a Book of Common Prayer, composed by Archbishop Cranmer, which has been described as one of the Church's 'priceless jewels'. Its prayers could be heard and the parson seen far more clearly by the congregation as the normal Sunday morning service was now Mattins and was conducted from a reading desk and pulpit at the top of the nave. The chancel was only used for an occasional Communion Service, conducted not at the old altar at the east end by a priest dressed in colourful vestments, but by a minister dressed simply in a surplice at a new communion table in the middle of the chancel, round which sat the communicants.

Moreover, parsons were allowed to marry and were expected to be men of learning, as they were now 'ministers of the word', who had to be capable of explaining the Christian faith to their parishioners. Their sermons and the official prayers were regarded as all-important. Consequently, anything that might distract the attention of the congregation, like wall paintings, statues or stained glass, had to be got rid of. The only decoration allowed was a large black panel above the chancel arch on which was inscribed in gold the Creed, the Lord's Prayer and the Ten Commandments.

The one check to these changes came in the short reign of Elizabeth's half-sister, Mary (1553-58), when there was a return to Papal Supremacy, with the Latin Mass, altars and vestments restored. But with the Queen's early death, they quickly vanished.

At St Mary's the enforcement of so much radical change led to a great deal of destruction. The two Churchwardens in 1553, John Child, a prosperous farmer, and John Wight, 'a gentleman', had to find money to pay for 'the taking down the altars' and the paving of the floor where they had stood; in their place they had to buy an expensive communion table, covered by a carpet. They also had to hire workmen to 'whiten' the wall paintings and to 'mend' the windows after some at least of the stained glass had been removed. In addition they had to buy the new service books and send the old ones to Croydon. To meet all these

---

INVENTORY OF CHURCH GOODS, DECEMBER 1552

Vestments:	9 Chasubles	2 white – 1 'white satin of Bridges', i.e. Bruges.
		1 'blue damask'; 1 violet.
		2 red – 1 'red and black silk'.
		3 green – 1 'green silk with the name Alice Wyche on it'.

'And all things to them', including alb, stole and 'head-piece', i.e. amice.
Cope of crimson velvet, 'wrought with gold'.

Plate:	2 Chalices, with patens 'parcel gilt'
	2 Crosses of 'copper and gilt';.
Altar materials:	Hanging altar cloths of silk; 6 altar cloths.
	2 Fringes, one with 'heads of silk and gold'
	'Veil Cloth' (for Lent)
	2 Sepulchre cloths 'of coarse cloth of gold'.
	1 Cruet of tin.
At doors:	2 Holy Water 'stooks', one of lead, the other of 'latten', i.e. brass.
In 'the Steeple':	3 'Belles'. Also Hand Bell, Sacring Bell and 'Sauns Bell'.
Stolen:	1 vestment; 1 cope; 1 surplice; 1 cruet of tin; 2 old crosses; brass lamp; brass senser;
	4 brass candlesticks; herse cloth; 'cere' cloth of silk.
	Bible

Lingard   Edwyn Lingard the sonne of Wm Lyngard and Elizabeth his wiffe was buried the xvij of July 1603

Symson   Mary Symson the daughter of Wm Symson and of Mary his wiffe was buried the xviij of July 1603

Symson   William Symson was buried the xxe of July 1603

Cotton   John Cotton the sonne of John Cotton and of Katheryne his wiffe was buried the xxvij of July 1603

Hond   Margery Hond was buried the xxviij of July 1603

Chamberlaine   Jacob Chamberlaine was buried the 3 of August 1603

Lingard   Wm Lyngard was buried the 4th of August 1603

Symson   Wm Symson the sonne of Wm Symson & Mary his wiffe was buried the vth of August 1603

Metam   John Metam was buried the vijth of August 1603

Lyngard   Elizabeth Lingard the daughter of Wm Lyngard and of Elizabeth his wiffe was buried the xvijth of August 1603

Lingard   Wm Lingard and Richard Lingard ye sonnes of Wm Lingard and of Elizabeth his wiffe buried the xxth of August 1603

Lingard   John Lingard ye sonne of William Lingard & of Elizabeth his wiffe buried the xxijth of August 1603

Wright   Wm Wright was buried the xxvth of August 1603

Buck   John Buck was buried the 4th of September 1603

Lingard   Anne Lingard sonne of Wm Lingard and of Elizabeth his wiffe was buried the ixth of September 1603

Lingard   Dorothy Lingard daughter of William Lingard and of Eliz his wiffe buried the xvth of September 1603

'The register of all the Buriwalls which have beene in the parish of Wimbledon' did not start until 1593. This extract is from ten years later, when in the summer of 1603 it had to record an unprecedented number of deaths, almost entirely due to the plague. One family, the Lingards, was nearly wiped out. William (who ran the corn mill on the Wandle) and seven of his children died in just two months. Only his wife Elizabeth and a baby boy survived.

expenses, they sold the stone altars, the candlesticks and some of the vestments (Wight bought one, as did other leading villagers, perhaps to keep them in case of a return of 'the old ways'). The most valuable church property – the chalices, the silk altar cloths and the three bells in the steeple – were taken by the government, though it could not get hold of a lot of other goods, including a cope and the Bible, as they had been 'stolen out of the church by night'. As the same excuse was given at many local churches, it seems probable that the Churchwardens arranged the 'burglary' as a cover to hide the goods from government agents.

Then as soon as the Catholic Mary Tudor took control, the old vestments came out of their hiding places, the old service books were returned, the altar was rebuilt

The monument to William and Katherine Walter on the north wall of the chancel, immediately on the left of the altar. It commemorates a local heiress, Katherine Lewston, and her husband, William Walter from Northamptonshire, who married in 1537. They owned a great deal of land, had seven children and lived to celebrate their golden wedding. William died in September 1587, Katherine only four months later. The family arms are above the monument.

and Latin Mass was again said in St Mary's. It is very doubtful if the priest who officiated was John Browne. In Edward's reign he had married twice and so he was only given permission to act as a priest again if he gave up his second wife and moved to a parish in Oxfordshire. His successor was Thomas Young about whom nothing is known. He may have said the Mass in St Mary's on Easter Sunday 1556 at which Sir William Cecil's Secretary listed 'the names of them in the parish of Wembletoun that was confessed and received the sacrament of the altar'. Almost the entire adult population of the village, about 150, were there.

Soon after the accession of Elizabeth I, however, the Mass was again banned and Protestant services restored. The Churchwardens had to take down the new altar, get rid of the vestments once more and put back the communion table. How much money these changes, on top of those under Mary, cost the parish is not known as the Churchwardens' accounts for the two reigns have not survived. But there can be little doubt that parishioners were now wary of spending anything on the church. At least there was none of the sad destruction seen in Edward's reign. Elizabeth wanted 'decent order' in her Church, and insisted that the screen separating nave from chancel should be kept, though without the rood.

The reaction of the parishioners at St Mary's to all the changes is unknown, though one important landowner, William Walter, and his wife Katherine had clearly become sincere Protestants by the time they died (just before the Armada arrived, as is shown by their fine monument on the north wall of the chancel). The rest of the congregation seem to have continued going to church, no matter what service they attended. But there can be little doubt that their traditional beliefs would have been shaken, as well as their respect for the clergy and for their parish church. Gifts to the church rapidly dried up and so the Churchwardens had to pay for repairs by levying a Church Rate. By the late 1620s with more gentlemen settling in the Wimbledon area, they were able to raise the money to build a gallery 'at the further end of the church near the belfry' to seat 'some of the better sort of parishioners' who were prepared to pay for the privilege of a family pew. But they were unable to repair the timber steeple which 'standeth upon the top of the church most poorly'. The manor steward promised to rebuild it in brick, but then did nothing.

In such circumstances the task of the Churchwardens was far more onerous than it had been in previous centuries. Moreover, they were given extra duties by the government, especially looking after 'vagabonds' and the 'casual' poor. From 1599 their names begin to appear in the Parish Register which they often seem to have kept for the minister. In the 1630s, for instance, Tobias Fenton, a yeoman, made neat, clear entries, whereas Thomas Sargent, a gentleman, 'registered no infants' for four years. But a third, Thomas Round, just after starting his year of office, 'with two of his sons and a daughter died of the plague'.

A 'Preaching Ministry' under Charles I

The position of the parson was also very difficult. He was now virtually a servant of the Cecil family who lived first at the Rectory and after 1588 at their new manor house on the slope to the east of the church. In a confidential letter to Archbishop Laud in 1637, the Vicar was described as the ' household chaplain' who 'reads prayers thrice a day in the house, attends at meals and when he hath done, eats with the servants'. His salary was a mere £20 (instead of the £200 that the tithes should have given him), supplemented with the offerings

---

THE CECIL CHAPEL

Built in the late 1620s, it was meant to be a mortuary chapel for the lord of the manor, Sir Edward Cecil, Viscount Wimbledon, and his family.

In the centre is the Viscount's large black altar tomb. Flat and without an effigy, it is inscribed with an outline of his career and his 'assured hope in his Saviour Christ to rise again to Glory Everlasting'. Above it there used to hang a Viscount's coronet, but this (together with militia armour on the wall) was stolen some years ago.

On the floor near the tomb are three other gravestones: of his second wife, Diana; his grand-daughter, Frances Ellis; and another grand-daughter's husband, Richard Betenson, who had lived at Eagle House.

On the walls are five small marble tablets: to his first wife, Theodosia; his second, Diana; his daughters, Frances and Elizabeth, and their husbands, Hon. James Fiennes and Lord Francis Willhoughby; his daughter, Albinia, and her husband, Sir Christopher Wray; and his daughter, Dorothy, 'unmaryed as yet'. Above the tablets are small windows, each with the Cecil arms, combined with those of the husbands.

The chapel is lit by a Perpendicular-style window in the south wall. It contains not merely the Cecil arms, but the only piece of medieval stained glass in the church, a fifteenth-century figure of St George, which was once in the chancel.

The Cecil Chapel photographed in 1921, before the
Clergy Vestry partly blocked the bottom half of the
window, and before the armour and coronet were stolen
in the 1970s. (*left*) Sir Edward Cecil, Baron Putney and
Viscount Wimbledon (1571-1638). In this engraving he
is shown as a 'Generall'. He fought in the Netherlands
and led an unsuccessful attack on Cadiz in 1625.

HIS FIRST WIFE WHO IN THIS
TOMBE IS NAMED :

HIS SECOND WIFE :

The large Perpendicular window in the Cecil Chapel. The stained glass on its left shows
the arms of Sir Thomas Cecil, Earl of Exeter, father of Viscount Wimbledon. The picture
of St George on the right is the oldest stained glass in the church; it dates from the
fifteenth century and was originally on the north side of the chancel.

The tablet to Viscount
Wimbledon's second daughter,
'Dorothey Cecill unmaryed as
yet'. It was originally on the
west wall of the Chapel, but in
1920 was moved to the south
wall of the Warrior Chapel.
Dorothy died in France in
1652, still unmarried. She left
money to found a charity to
help the poor of Wimbledon.

DOROTHEY CECILL VNMARYED
AS YET

at Easter and fees for baptisms, marriages and funerals which at Wimbledon did not amount to much.

It is therefore hardly surprising that St Mary's no longer attracted ambitious clerics. Indeed, no record has survived even of the names of most of the Elizabethan Vicars. The last one, Richard Townson (*c*1601-1604), later became famous as a preacher, Dean of Westminster and Bishop of Salisbury. But it was not until the reign of Charles I and the arrival of the Revd Christopher Fox in about 1630 that the congregation at St Mary's 'constantly enjoyed the happiness of a preaching ministry' at services where the centrepiece was the sermon. By then the dignified words of the English Liturgy and of the English Bible heard Sunday after Sunday would certainly have had an effect on parishioners who had by law to go to the service and there 'abide soberly'.

Like all the Vicars until the 1860s, Fox, a Cambridge MA, had to live in lodgings; in 1649 he shared a small cottage near the church with the French gardener at the manor house. Though regarded by Edward Cecil, Viscount Wimbledon, as 'Mr Fox, my chaplain', he seems to have won a following in the village through his ability as a preacher. Only six years after his arrival, there was a request from parishioners for an increase in his stipend and in 1641 the request was repeated, again without success. Still, one lady left him money in her will 'to make a sermon once a year in the parish church of Wimbledon so long as he liveth there'. Another, Mrs Knox, mother of a famous seaman, lived in the village throughout Fox's ministry and must have been one of his supporters. According to her son, she had 'God in all her thoughts' and taught him 'to love, fear and serve God, to read in the Bible' and to say his prayers regularly.

In 1638 Fox would have officiated at the funeral of 'Lord Wimbledon of Wimbledon'. In his will, witnessed by the minister who received the welcome legacy of ten pounds, the last Cecil lord of the manor had asked to be buried in the parish church, 'in the special chapel and tomb where my second wife lies', but 'with as little ceremony as possible'. The chapel survives as the only visible reminder of the presence of the Cecil family in Wimbledon.

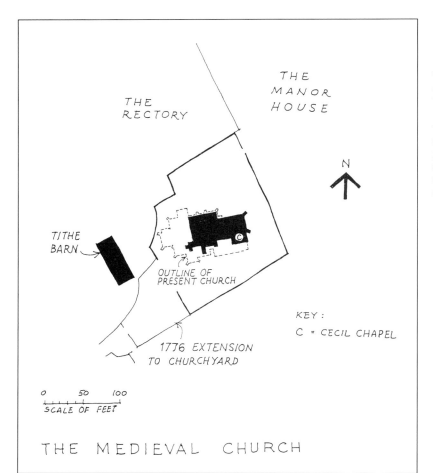

THE
MANOR
HOUSE

THE
RECTORY

N

TITHE
BARN

OUTLINE OF
PRESENT CHURCH

KEY :

C = CECIL CHAPEL

1776 EXTENSION
TO CHURCHYARD

0   50   100

SCALE OF FEET

THE MEDIEVAL CHURCH

This plan is based on the earliest known map of Wimbledon, drawn in the 1720s. It shows the church with its very small nave, its size compared with the present building, and its small churchyard whose original wall only survives on the east and south.

This painting of the medieval church was made about 1780 by John Barralet. It looks a more presentable building than in the 1796 engraving, but is hardly a worthy church for a fashionable village. The end of the tithe barn is on the left, the parson (probably Herbert Randolph) is just beyond the churchyard wall, while the 1776 extension of the churchyard is on the right.

THE CIVIL WAR AND AFTER

Effect of the Civil Wars

The building of the Cecil Chapel and the burial there of Viscount Wimbledon marked the virtual end of an era in the history of St Mary's. The Viscount's widow promptly put the manor house and park on the market and they were bought by Charles I's wife, Henrietta Maria, as a home for her mother, Marie de Medici. Henrietta probably never visited Wimbledon, but the fact that the 'Papist Queen' had valuable property in the area ensured that the village could not escape involvement in the disputes between King and Parliament, particularly after the royal family left London in January 1642.

Services at St Mary's seem to have carried on as normal throughout the first Civil War, despite the presence of Parliamentary troops in the village. Christopher Fox, however, was no longer answerable to the Archbishop of Canterbury. Bishops were abolished in 1643 and Archbishop Laud was in the Tower charged with treason. Instead, Wimbledon formed part of a local presbytery in north-eastern Surrey, presided over by the minister at Kingston, Dr Staunton.

In 1646 as the first War came to an end, the effect on religion of Parliament's victory became even clearer. Use of the Anglican Book of Common Prayer was banned and services now had to be taken from the Presbyterian Directory of Public Worship. Then after the triumph of the New Model Army and the execution of the King in 1649, the new Republican or Commonwealth government began promoting 'godliness and virtue'. The celebration of Christmas, Shrove Tuesday and Whitsun was banned as a 'relic of Popery'. Drunkeness and blaspheming were to be severely punished, along with 'profane walking', opening the front gate on the Sabbath for any purpose except to go to church. To confuse people further, marriage became a civil ceremony before a local magistrate.

No record has survived of any Wimbledonian being punished for 'ungodliness'. But all were affected by a further reform, introduced by Oliver Cromwell in 1654 shortly after he became Lord Protector. A sincerely religious man, he was concerned over the quality of the ministers in many parishes. So he set up a Commission of Triers and Ejectors to test the suitability of every parson. Its immediate effect on St Mary's was just what many of the congregation had been demanding for twenty years. Christopher Fox's stipend was increased first to sixty and then to eighty pounds. In addition, he lost his theoretical responsibility for Putney and Mortlake, which at long last became separate parishes.

In 1656, however, the Commissioners ruined the effect of these reforms. Without giving any reasons for their judgement, they declared that they were 'not satisfied of the Revd Christopher Fox's fitness to serve the cure of Wimbledon' and asked the new lord of the manor, General John Lambert, 'to nominate some fit person'. Lambert did nothing, but when he was out of favour with Cromwell two years later, the Commissioners stepped in and themselves nominated Revd William Syms. Fox had to leave Wimbledon after nearly thirty years as its minister and is never heard of again.

Revd William Syms and the Restoration

Nothing also is known of his successor's early life or why he was chosen to serve St Mary's. Syms was certainly an extreme Puritan and was linked to the Millenarians who almost daily awaited the second coming of the Lord which they saw predicted in 'signs and portents; – the death of Oliver Cromwell (which happened only a few months after Syms's arrival in Wimbledon), 'a bright cloud dropping fire on Whitehall' and even 'three suns seen near Kingston'.

A minister with such a background could hardly fail to antagonise the very conservative congregation at St Mary's. Not merely had he displaced a well-liked parson, but his style of preaching would not have appealed to them. So, shortly after the Restoration of Charles II in May 1660, one of the Churchwardens 'hindered him from preaching in the public place', in other words stopped him taking the service at St Mary's. Syms retorted by holding a service at his own house on Southside. Tempers then became heated and one of the villagers, Nathaniel Pace, 'did most bitterly rail against Mr Syms and his meeting'. But soon afterwards, according to Syms's supporters, Pace died from a stroke, 'raving, cursing and swearing'.

To calm the atmosphere, the parson at Mortlake was asked to take the services, but seems to have died before he could visit Wimbledon. Then in 1662 Parliament passed a new Act of Uniformity requiring all ministers to use a revised Book of Common Prayer and take an oath of loyalty to the King. Syms refused to do either and was at last officially ejected from the church. But he stayed in the parish, living in a very reasonable house on

VICARS, 1630–1739	
1630	Christopher Fox, MA
1658	William Syms
1661*	Edward Lyford
1663	Thomas Luckeyn, MA
1665	Humphrey Williams, MA
1668*	Thomas Wilmot, MA
1671	Thomas Jones, MA
1684	Edward Collins, MA (to 1739)

* Extra names found since the list in the church was made

The three oldest Communion Cups owned by the church: on the right, a silver gilt cup
of 1562; on the left the Wilbraham cup of 1665; in the centre a silver gilt flagon, 'a
gift to ye Communion Table of the Parish of Wimbledon in Surrey. February 6, 1715'.

Southside and on friendly terms with his neighbours. He continued preaching
at secret conventicles in Ewell and Kingston, though never apparently in
Wimbledon. He was regularly fined for not attending his parish church, yet had
four of his children baptised at St Mary's and when he died in 1685 was buried
in its graveyard. With his death the short history of Nonconformity in Wimbledon
virtually came to an end, not to be revived for another hundred years.

In the meantime the country was trying to settle down under a restored
monarchy and Church of England. Unfortunately Charles II's reign began with

three major disasters: the Great Plague of 1665, the Fire of London the following year and the Dutch fleet in the Medway in 1667. It ended in the early 1680s with a major crisis: an attempt by the new Whig party to place the Duke of Monmouth, one of the King's illegitimate sons, on the throne. It was also far from settled in religion with the restored bishops excluding Puritans from the church and persecuting the Quakers.

Services at St Mary's were equally unsettled under three short-lived parsons.

EARLY GRAVESTONES

Inside St Mary's there are two interesting seventeenth-century gravestones. The first is at the top of the nave, just in front of the gates leading into the chancel. Under the matting is a large black stone slab with an inscription in Latin commemorating Sir Richard Wynn MP who died in July 1649. He was Henrietta Maria's treasurer and throughout the Civil Wars had stayed at Wimbledon trying to protect the Queen's fine manor house and park from marauding soldiers. He finally collapsed under the strain and died only a few months after the execution of Charles I.

The second is under a carpet on the floor of the Warrior Chapel. It covers the vault of the Pitt family (apparently not related to the famous Prime Minister). The first Pitt buried there was Thomas, a prosperous merchant of the Africa Company. He owned property in London and Essex, as well as in Wimbledon where in 1691 he bought a house on Southside, with two orchards. He died in April 1699. Nine other members of the family were later buried or commemorated in the vault, the last an Ensign in the Coldstream Guards, killed in April 1814 in one of the last battles of the Peninsular War.

In the churchyard there are two early headstones, let into the vestry wall. The earliest is for 'Mr J. Simpson, a zealous minister of Jesus Christ, blest in the conversion of very many souls in the City of London'. He died in 1662. He was buried here because in Tudor times the Simpsons had been one of the most prosperous yeomen families in the village, living in a cottage about where the Rose and Crown Inn is today. John, the eighth of nine children, was born there in 1587.

Near his headstone is one commemorating Wimbledon's first known butcher, Phanuel Maybank. It is decorated with an hour-glass, skull, pickaxe and shovel, and records his death 'in the sixty-fifth year of his age'. Phanuel came from Kingston in 1645 at the height of the Civil War. He opened a shop, married, had eight children and prospered. At his death he was as wealthy as a yeoman farmer.

Sir Richard Wynn, Queen Henrietta Maria's Treasurer.

(*below*) The tombstone of Phanuel Maybank, Wimbledon's first known butcher.

Hear Lieth interred the body of
Phanuel Maybank of this Parish
who Departed this life may the
22 Anno Dom 1684
and in the 64 yeare of his

In 1663 the first, Thomas Luckeyn, was put in prison for failing to arrest the new lord of the manor, the Earl of Bristol, who had accused Charles II's chief minister, the Earl of Clarendon, of high treason, then dared to appear in the parish church before riding away into hiding. His successor, Humphrey Williams, had the unusual habit of entering all baptisms in Latin in the Parish Register, keeping English for burials. The third Vicar, Thomas Wilmot, a young man of twenty-three, only lasted a year, before going off to take his MA at Cambridge. He was replaced by Thomas Jones who came in 1671 with the recommendation that he was 'proficient in learning, a constant preacher'. He stayed longer than his three predecessors, twelve years, and then in December 1683 suddenly died, leaving forty-five pounds 'unto five and forty poor French Protestants that came into England for their religion's sake', refugees from Louis XIV's persecution.

During the twenty years, 1663-1683, that these four parsons took the services, several significant events occurred at St Mary's. First in 1665, the year of the Great Plague, Ralph Wilbraham, a City merchant and a possible victim, was buried in the chancel. In his memory, a chalice was given to the Vicar by his widow Anne for use in the Communion Service; it is still in use today. Then two years later three labourers, 'being wicked and depraved persons, played at nine pins' instead of going to church. They were fined three shillings and four pence by the local magistrates and so became the last Wimbledonians to be accused of such a crime, since after the Toleration Act of 1689 no-one could be forced to go to church. Finally, one Sunday in 1683 a violent argument broke out in St Mary's between two leading landowners, Joseph Lawrence and Thomas Morris, who each claimed the right to occupy the same pew in the gallery. The dispute was taken to court and finally settled well over a year later. It was a foretaste of worse disputes to come under the next minister, Edward Collins.

Revd Edward Collins and the Hanoverians

In many ways Collins was typical of ministers chosen in the following hundred years to serve parishes all over England. He was a young MA (from Oxford) with a good knowledge of theology, recently ordained and expecting to stay in his new parish for the rest of his life. Collins certainly remained at St Mary's for a record fifty-five years – from his appointment early in 1684 until April 1739 when an unknown parson recorded in the Register: 'Mr Edward Collins, minister of this parish, was buried'.

His years at St Mary's spanned some dramatic events: the Revolution of 1688

An extract from the Parish Register for 1723 – the Revd Edward Collins's entry for the baptism of a poor woman's baby. It starts on the previous page: 'July 2. Susanna, daughter of Moses and Mary Cooper, travellers, born in Martin [Merton] and the poor woman being desirous to have it baptised . . .' It is the longest entry in the Register and reflects great credit on Collins, who was Vicar of both Wimbledon and Merton. (*See page* 49).

when William III and his wife Mary replaced the Catholic James II on the throne; two major wars with Louis XIV's France which enabled Britain to become one of the Great Powers of Europe; and the succession in 1714 of the ruler of Hanover, George I, and the attempt in the next year by James II's son, 'the Old Pretender', to displace him. Yet barely a mention of these changes appears in the church records, above all in the Vicar's letters which are almost entirely taken up with his need for money.

Collins was typical of the many poorer parsons whose annual income of fifty pounds or less should have qualified them from 1704 to benefit from Queen Anne's Bounty. Collins's stipend as Perpetual Curate was only forty pounds (the increase during the Protectorate had been nullified at the Restoration). He also earned an extra ten pounds for preaching a special sermon, as well as a little from the Easter Offerings and church fees. But as the Rectory was permanently leased to the lord of the manor, he had to use some of his small income to rent a cottage in the village where he could bring up his ever-growing family (four sons and four daughters, born between 1685 and 1697) and 'keep a school' to help pay for their food and clothes. Early in the next century he was greatly helped by Sir Theodore Janssen, soon to be lord of the manor, who allowed him to use his fine new mansion at the corner of Church Road and the High Street rent free. Then in 1712 he became Vicar of St Mary's Merton as well and the combined income from the two parishes raised him into 'the middling sort' of Anglican parson.

Yet his financial troubles were far from over. Between 1717 and 1725 he wrote a series of ever more desperate letters to the lord of the manor and the Dean of Worcester (the official Rector of Wimbledon) begging for help. To the Dean he protested that though Janssen regarded him as 'a good preacher and tolerable good man', yet in 1718 he had turned him and his family out of the house in Church Road, wrongly claiming they were Jacobites because they wore white roses on the Pretender's birthday, and on King George's birthday 'put out the bonfire on the Common'. His next source of trouble was 'my abused daughter' whom he tried to defend in a lawsuit which cost him an entire year's income. As a result, in 1721 he tried to raise money by increasing the fees for baptisms, marriages and burials without consulting his Churchwardens. They promptly denounced him to the Archbishop. By 1725 he was almost in despair, writing to the Dean: 'I have not a shilling to command. At the worst of times I was never in greater straits than now.' He claimed he was short of food and fuel,

The vault covering the tomb of Sir Theodore Janssen, 'once Lord of this Manor', who died in 1748. It is in the centre of the picture, now only made of brick, but originally covered with stone.

and could not pay his bills, especially for cheese, butter and bacon from a London cheesemonger 'who pressed hard for money'. The Dean made him a small loan which seems to have tided him over the immediate crisis and perhaps enabled him to set his financial affairs straight. Certainly no more begging letters have survived from his last fourteen years at St Mary's.

In addition to his financial troubles and disputes with Janssen and the Church-wardens, Collins had problems with other important parishioners. He almost seems to have got himself involved in a power-struggle to reassert the parson's right to control his church. Two men in particular infuriated him, Peter Lordell and William Browne. Lordell was a wealthy merchant who lived at Lingfield House on Southside. Collins claimed he was 'one of my greatest enemies', yet the only dispute he ever mentioned was over the family tomb 'under the communion table'. There is no lack of detail, however, on his relations with 'the vexatious and wicked Browne', as he was forced to take him to court. Like Lordell, Browne was a wealthy London merchant who bought the three hundred acre Old Park estate west of the Common and there built Westside House for himself and the original Cannizaro which he leased to friends. In 1722 he got up at a meeting of the Vestry and alluding to Collins's recent attempt to increase fees for services, accused him of being 'a rogue, a robber of the church and a cozener of the poor, who ought to have his gown pulled over his ears'. Then on eight successive Sundays he ostentatiously left his pew as soon as Collins got into the pulpit, 'clapt the door after him with very great force' and walked out 'in a very irreverent and indecent manner'. (At Merton parish church another difficult character, Justice Meriton, was insulting the minister in exactly the same way.) Collins

Another extract from the Parish Register: an entry for 'Briefs', a list of collections made in 1692 after appeals for 'good causes'. Two parish churches – Chagford in Devon and Havant in Hampshire – only received about ten shillings each. But an appeal for 'ye Redemption of ye Captives in Algiers, Sally, Barbary etc.' raised the very large sum of £12.16.0. The accounts are signed by the minister and Churchwardens.

took Browne to court, accusing him not merely of disturbing the services, but of 'cohabiting with Anne Needham' and 'abusing their neighbours in most scandalous language'. The case lasted a year and Browne was duly excommunicated. Nonetheless, when he died in January 1738, Collins gave him a Christian burial in St Mary's churchyard, but in the Register he added a mysterious four letter word, 'dung'.

Despite all his troubles, Collins kept the Parish Register himself with meticulous care for over fifty years. Towards the end the writing deteriorated and for the first time a Mr Griffiths conducted some of the marriages. Otherwise Collins ran the parish entirely on his own and yet found time to give the occupations of many of those he buried (for which later historians are in his debt). He even added the strange story of two 'travellers' Moses and Mary Cooper, who came to Merton Church during morning service to ask him to baptise their baby daughter. They were promptly arrested by Justice Meriton who threatened to send the husband to a House of Correction if they did not leave the district at once. The Coopers, however, found out that Collins was also Vicar of Wimbledon and brought the child to his lodgings in the village, where he duly baptised her.

During his long stay at St Mary's, Collins preached innumerable sermons. Every year some had to be devoted to 'Briefs' – appeals for good causes. Most seem to have left his congregation unmoved, notably one for a church in Yorkshire which raised less than two shillings 'besides a groat with a hole in it'. But an appeal in 1692 'for the redemption of the captives in Algiers, Sally, Barbary etc.' raised nearly thirteen pounds, while another twelve years later 'for the widows and orphans of seamen that were drowned in the storm' (the previous November when twelve warships went down off the Scilly Isles) produced just under eight pounds. His Churchwardens too seem to have kept St Mary's in a reasonable state. A typical report is that made by Lancelot Thackstone and John Drewry in 1685. 'We having our church in good order – and not having any Dissenters in our parish.' There was clearly much more to Collins's long ministry at St Mary's than troubles over money and disputes with members of his congregation.

PART THREE

The Georgian Church

The Spencers and St Mary's

The arrival at Wimbledon Park House in the spring of 1756 of John Spencer (later the first Earl) and his young wife Georgiana signalled a new era both for the village and the church. For the previous thirty years there had been no resident lord of the manor to act as a centre of local society and as a support to the Vicar in matters of religion. To make the situation worse, St Mary's during most of this time had been served by an elderly, disillusioned parson. So it is hardly surprising that about the middle of the eighteenth century the church in Wimbledon seemed at a low ebb as the Church of England seemed to be all over the country.

Over the next seventy years, until they gave up the manor house in 1827, the Spencer family helped to transform the place. At St Mary's they 'set so very good an example that Divine Service is very well attended'. Every Sunday when they were in residence (normally for a few weeks in the spring, summer and early autumn), they came to morning service. They sat in a special box pew with glass in the door, covered by green silk curtains, a carpet on the floor and a fire-place to keep them warm.

Georgian services, normally Mattins, have been described as 'somnolent' and as 'testing the patience of worshippers'. They were taken from the 1662 Book of Common Prayer, but there were no hymns, only metrical psalms and a long uninspiring sermon. 'The Sacrament of the Lord's Supper' was celebrated 'not more than four times a year' – at Christmas, Easter, Whitsun and Michaelmas – but there were few communicants. At St Mary's the morning service started about eleven and was 'seldom over till near one o'clock'. In the summer there

VICARS, 1739–1846		
1739	John Cooksey, MA	Fellow of the Royal Society
1777	Herbert Randolph, MA	Fellow of Magdalen, Oxford; Precentor of St Paul's
1819	Henry Lindsay, MA	(to 1846)

George Spencer, the second Earl (1758-1834) with (*below*), an extract from the Parish Register recording his baptism in October 1758.

morris. William son of John ...
wife was baptized Au...

Ross. James son of James B...
was baptized August ...

Gilbert. Elizabeth daughter ...
Elizabeth his wife was l...

Burypin. Thomas son of Thom...
his wife was baptized ...

Hoard. Joseph son of Foster ... 5758

Maitland. wife was baptized August the 27...
Charles son of Alexander Maitland ...
Edyth his wife was baptized Septr. the 3d. 5758.

Chaney. Sarah daughter of William Chaney, & Mary
his wife was baptized October the 8th. 5758.

Spencer. George John, son of John Spencer Esqr.
and Georgiana his wife; he was born Septemr.
the first, & baptized October the sixteenth. 1758
His majesty, & Earl Cowper being Godfathers.
The Duchess of Marlborough, & Lady Dowager
Bateman Godmothers. It is remarkable that
His majesty George the second, was godfather not
only to this young Gentleman, but to his mother
daughter of the Hon: Stephen Poyntz Esqr, and to
his Grandmother daughter of the Right Hon:
The Earl of Granville.

A painting of the Georgian church from the west, made by H. Petrie in 1801. It shows a more fashionable building with large regular windows – and on the extreme right a small building with a curved roof whose purpose is unknown.

was also an evening service; in the winter this had to be given up as the church had neither lights nor heat – and the box-pews were the only means of keeping out draughts. Yet despite the fact that it was no longer compulsory to attend the service, St Mary's was full almost every Sunday (the rest of the week it was kept locked). In 1758 the Vicar was even able to claim that he knew of none who 'profess to disregard religion or who commonly absent themselves from all public worship on Sundays'.

This parson was John Cooksey who succeeded Collins in 1739 and served the parish for nearly forty years. He seems to have been more optimistic and level-headed than Collins; he was certainly better off financially. A member of an old Worcestershire family, an Oxford MA and a Fellow of the Royal Society, he was Rector of a City church (which he served in the winter), as well as Vicar of Wimbledon, and later secured a third parish in Essex. He was therefore able to live as a gentleman parson, leasing a fine new house near the Common. He was said to have been 'a diligent minister, methodical and kindly', and seems to have looked after the parish well, though in his last years his health was poor.

He worked closely with the first Earl Spencer and his Countess in a matter for which all three cared deeply – the education of the poor. Cooksey revived the Cecil Charity, founded a century before by Viscount Wimbledon's daughter, Dorothy, to help poor boys to learn to read and write, and enable them to become apprentices. Countess Georgiana helped many of the children; her husband became one of the Charity Trustees. In 1758 Cooksey proposed the building of a Free School for poor children. The Earl allowed it to be put up on the Common and gave a large sum towards the first school-house (which still stands in Camp Road), while his wife provided 'handsomely bound Bibles' and Prayer Books as prizes for hard-working boys and girls.

When Cooksey died in 1777, his successor, Herbert Randolph, seemed even more distinguished. His father was Vice-Chancellor of Oxford University; a younger brother was Professor of Poetry at Oxford and later a Bishop; he himself was a Fellow of Magdalen College. Like Cooksey, he seems to have been accepted

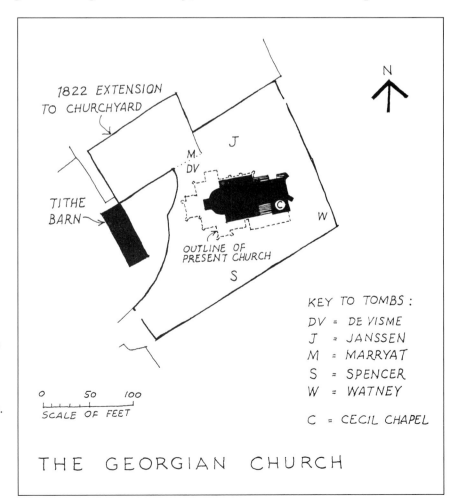

The chief addition to the church is the western apse, while the churchyard has been extended into the Rectory grounds.

1822 EXTENSION TO CHURCHYARD

TITHE BARN

OUTLINE OF PRESENT CHURCH

J

M. DV

W

S

KEY TO TOMBS:
DV = DE VISME
J = JANSSEN
M = MARRYAT
S = SPENCER
W = WATNEY

C = CECIL CHAPEL

0   50   100
SCALE OF FEET

THE GEORGIAN CHURCH

as a social equal by his many distinguished parishioners, who included not only the Spencers, but several cabinet ministers, peers, MPs, directors of the East India Company and judges. He lodged in two very comfortable houses, first on the Green and later on Westside. Yet he never appeared contented. Like Collins, he constantly complained about his low stipend and lack of a Vicarage, which meant he had to take on a second parish in Essex and so had to be away for two months every year.

Randolph was a worthy man who did his duty. But he seems to have inspired little enthusiasm in his congregation, even among the Spencer family. Six years after his arrival at St Mary's, the first Earl died and was succeeded by his only son George. The new Earl had been born at the manor house, baptised in the parish church and had grown up with a genuine love for the district. Through his mother's strong influence, he was also genuinely religious, went regularly to church and read a chapter of the Bible every day. He particularly liked a good sermon. On Easter Sunday 1780 at St Mary's he heard 'an excellent sermon, excellently preached', which led him 'to receive the Sacrament' and left him feeling 'much better for it all day'. The preacher was not the Vicar, but a family friend, the Bishop of St Asaph.

Sadly, Randolph was never in the same class. 'To church and heard as usual a very long and rather dull discourse from Mr Randolph' was a typical comment from the kindly Earl. His wife Lavinia was far more scathing: 'I never heard so stupid a sermon as good Mr Randolph gave us'. She promptly nicknamed him 'Snorum' or 'Snorman', while her eldest daughter, Sarah, referred to him as 'Randolfetto'. Perhaps as a result of such uninspiring sermons, the Vicar was forced to report to his archbishop in 1788 that 'public worship has not been so well attended as could have been wished'.

Johnson's New Church

Randolph hoped that attendance would improve when the church was enlarged. In July 1785 the Vestry had decided to add a north aisle to St Mary's. They had often been assured by the Churchwardens that the 500-year-old church was 'in good repair'. But with the population steadily growing it had become 'much crowded' and room for more seats was essential.

The architect chosen to carry out the work was John Johnson, County Surveyor of Essex, who had just finished adding an extra storey to a large mansion near the church (known later as Belvedere House). To the Vestry's sorrow he soon found 'the whole fabric and the roof in particular so much worse than expected' and advised major repairs to the south aisle before any extension was started. He then discovered that the north wall and steeple were also 'considerably out of repair'. So he told the Vestry that the only solution was to pull down the whole of the old nave and build a new one (the chancel had to be left, as it was the responsibility of the Archbishop of Canterbury). Reluctantly the Vestry agreed.

Rebuilding started early in 1787. Johnson wanted to employ his own workmen, but the Vestry insisted that local craftsmen be used. So William Jennings and William Terry, two experienced builders, started work, along with Samuel Mason, a carpenter (and also manager of the Rose and Crown) and Daniel Withem, a glazier. By Easter Monday they had made enough progress for the foundation stone to be laid by the Vicar. From then on, however, work proceeded more slowly than expected, partly because it was decided to raise the floor nearly two feet to make the building 'more wholesome and free from damps'. The rest of the year passed and half the next before the new church could be used for services, but it was not until January 1790 that Johnson was able to tell the Vestry that work was complete.

To judge from contemporary drawings, the Georgian church looked more impressive than its medieval predecessor. Built of grey brick, it had a wide nave

(*left*) A side view of the church by an unknown artist. (*right*) A painting of the church from the east, probably by John Buckler about 1810. It shows the door under the chancel window leading to the new vestry. Otherwise the outside of the medieval chancel is not affected by the rebuilding of the nave.

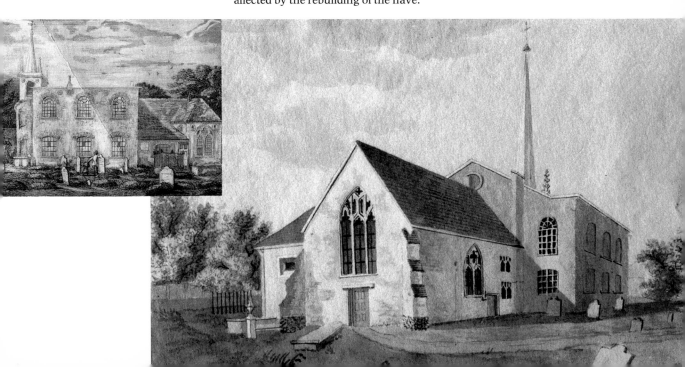

The Georgian chancel about 1810. A drawing by an unknown artist, showing the tiny apse with a high pulpit over the communion table and higher still the windows of the Spencer pew.

(*below*) The Chancel in 1825. A drawing by Gideon Yates. It shows the return to use of the full chancel, with the communion table and the black commandments board at the east end, new Spencer pews on either side and a new high pulpit to the right.

lit by two rows of round-headed windows. At the west end, a bowed entrance supported a square wooden tower, decorated with artificial stone pinnacles and surmounted by a copper spire (whose cost was met by 'a gentleman', later revealed as the Prime Minister, William Pitt, who attended services at St Mary's on his frequent visits to Wimbledon). The interior was said to have been 'fitted up in the Greek style', then fashionable among architects. At the east end the old chancel was transformed with a shallow plaster apse just inside the altar rails. In the tiny space were crowded the communion table, a very high pulpit and the reading desk, while the apse itself was decorated with the Ten Commandments, Creed and Lord's Prayer. The rest of the chancel was fitted out as a vestry, entered by a new door just underneath the old east window. Above the vestry an upper storey was created for the Spencer family pew with windows looking down the nave from over the communion table. (Thirty years later the apse was removed, the chancel reopened, the communion table placed at the traditional east end and the Spencers given a pew to one side.)

The rebuilt nave and the aisles were provided with new box pews for the village tradesmen and their families. Over the aisles were galleries, supported on iron columns painted to look like Siena marble, where sat 'the gentry'. Above, the roof was covered by a plaster vault, divided into a series of shallow domes decorated with medallions of Adam, Noah and the Apostles. At the back a new, typically Georgian, font (a shallow bowl on an elegant pedestal) was placed near the benches for the poor. At the top of the nave there was a large stove burning coal, the first heating system ever installed at St Mary's.

While the rebuilding was going on, services were apparently held in the chancel, though this too would have had to have been closed at some later stage. The first service in the new church took place on 6 July 1788. It was marred by the collapse of a temporary gallery put up at the west end for another innovation, a choir and small band of musicians. Fortunately no-one was severely injured, but many were badly bruised and their instruments damaged.

Johnson's new church cost a little over £2,100. Just over half was raised by a Church Rate; the rest came from a voluntary subscription with 'one of the most considerable' sums given by 'Mr Levi, the Jew, of Prospect Place'. But the building seems never to have been liked by its congregation. It was compared to 'a barn' or 'a Methodist meeting-house' and was dismissed by Countess Lavinia as 'the ugliest church I have ever seen'. It also proved to have been badly built. The roof soon began to settle and needed immediate repair. In 1818 the tower had to be shored up because of 'dilapidations'. The stove too gave a lot of trouble and after several changes two large 'patent hot-air stoves' burning coke proved more satisfactory. In June 1796 there was also a disturbing break-in, when thieves stole the parson's surplice, the carpet on the communion table and several prayer books, as well as damaging locks and fittings in the pews. Despite the offer of a large reward, the thieves were never caught.

In his new church Randolph did do something to make the services a little brighter. The Churchwardens bought music books and a pitch-pipe. Then in 1797 the first choir or 'church singers' was formed under the lead of a gardener to perform 'Psalmody' from a special Singing Gallery. In addition the three bells in the new tower (dating from about 1520, 1572 and 1715) rang more frequently. Not merely did they now tell the people when services were due to start or when someone in the village had died. They were sounded on 'days of national importance', such as Oak-Apple Day and November the Fifth, and to celebrate victories, including an unknown triumph of 'Nealson' in October 1799.

Randolph's swan-song came exactly ten years later with a special service to celebrate George III's Golden Jubilee. The King was now blind and his health precarious. Only a year later his mind finally gave way and his eldest son became Prince Regent. Yet in the fifty years since his accession in 1760 Britain had been

transformed, above all by new canals, turnpike roads and cotton factories. The country had also overcome the loss of its American Colonies and had begun to build a new overseas Empire after major wars with France. In 1809 the latest war, with Napoleonic France, was not going well, but six years later it was to end in decisive victory at Waterloo. Yet despite all the successes under George III, Lavinia Spencer strongly disapproved of the old King and told her husband that she simply went to St Mary's 'to set an example'. But 'the service was of a length only to be compared to the King's reign – and just as dull and uninteresting, thanks to Snorum's animated delivery'. The church, she added, was 'far from full'. The Vicar, however, was now happier with attendances at morning service, but still felt that there were not 'so many communicants as might be wished'.

The Georgian font, drawn by Gideon Yates in 1825.

The Georgian nave in 1825. A drawing by Gideon Yates. It shows the stove, the box pews, the new organ, the iron columns supporting the galleries and the medallions in the roof. In the front of the western gallery are a number of small inscriptions, probably recording the chief bequests to the poor.

REMAINS OF THE GEORGIAN CHURCH – AND ITS PARISHIONERS

Much of Johnson's nave, like the medieval chancel, survives under the Victorian flint-covering. Only the western end and the tower were completely pulled down. The grey bricks at the eastern end of the aisles can still be seen from the churchyard.

In the churchyard too are the graves of many leading parishioners who lived in Georgian Wimbledon. Just to the left of the path from the church to Fellowship House are two large Spencer tombs. One is of the second Earl's mother-in-law, the Countess of Lucan (whom he disliked); she lived on Southside and died in 1814. The other is of his youngest daughter, Lady Georgiana Quinn, who died in childbirth in 1823, aged only twenty-eight.

Two of the builders of the Georgian church are buried nearby. In the Watney vault at the south-eastern corner of the churchyard lies Samuel Mason, who married Mary Watney and died in 1810. Round the north side of the chancel in a large family tomb lies William Jennings who died in 1822.

Near the Jennings tomb are two unusual graves. The first is simply a broken flat stone lying on the ground, with the brief inscription: 'W.W. 1777. H.W. 1778'. It covers the grave of William Wilberforce's uncle William and aunt Hannah. They lived at Lauriston House, Southside, and left it to their nephew. The second is a large brick tomb with a plain stone top covering the vault of the Janssen family. Among the ten people buried there is Sir Theodore Janssen, 'once Lord of this Manor', who died in 1748.

Further west on a line with the church porch are two striking tombs. The first is a large stone pyramid, put up in 1797, the year Napoleon conquered Egypt. It marks the grave of Gerard de Visme who lived at Wimbledon Lodge, Southside. He left money for the annual repair of his tomb and for bread to be given to the poor 'in the winter months'. Just to the north is a large stone sarcophagus with a coat of arms, but no inscription. Inside lie buried eight members of the Marryat family, including Mrs Charlotte Marryat who died in 1854, but not her novelist son, Frederick.

Finally, just inside the porch under the tower is the finest monument in the church. It is the work of a leading early nineteenth-century sculptor, Sir Richard Westmacott, and shows James Perry seated, studying a bust of the famous Whig statesman, Charles James Fox. Perry was owner and editor of a radical newspaper, *The Morning Chronicle*. He also owned Wimbledon corn mill on the Wandle and from 1791 to 1811 lived nearby at Wandlebank House. On his death in 1821 his friends in the Whig Fox Clubs commissioned the monument 'in testimony of the zeal, courage and ability with which he advocated the principles of civil and religious liberty'.

(*above left*) The monument to James Perry. It is now in the west porch, but until the Warrior Chapel was built in 1920, it was inside the church at the end of the south aisle. (*above right*) The Spencer tombs: on the right (with the stone vase on the top), the Countess of Lucan; on the left (with the wreath on the side), Lady Georgiana Quinn. (*below*) The De Visme tomb.

Mrs Charlotte Marryat (1773-1854).

Evangelical Revival

Randolph left Wimbledon for good in 1810. His brother, now Bishop of London, appointed him first Rector of Hanwell in Middlesex and then Precentor of St Paul's. Technically he remained Vicar of Wimbledon until he died in 1819, but he left the parish entirely in the hand of young Curates, first Edward Bullock, then William Pritchard and finally Henry Lindsay.

The Spencer family were pleased. The Earl was at morning service soon after Bullock arrived and told his aged mother that though his sermon was 'nothing very remarkable', yet 'it looks as if we should be gainers by the change'. His wife was deeply impressed by an outside preacher, a Putney clergyman, whose sermon on Methodism was 'incomparably the best I ever heard anywhere. It lasted three-quarters of an hour, yet I was very sorry when it finished'.

Bullock deserves to be remembered as the parson who in 1810 persuaded the Vestry to buy an organ for St Mary's. It was the first in the church since the Reformation, as organs had only begun to reappear in Surrey churches in the late eighteenth century (All Saints, Kingston, for instance installed its first organ in 1793). It was paid for by a voluntary contribution of the parishioners. The money also covered the salary of an organist who was to teach the children of the Free School singing so that they could in future form the church choir.

Bullock also started a voluntary subscription to finance a series of sermons to be given by himself on Sunday afternoons or evenings. Thirty-one of the wealthier parishioners, including Earl and Countess Spencer, Justice Park, Lady Manners and even the Prince de Condé, a Roman Catholic, were ready to contribute. His example was followed by his successors and among their listeners was the Comte St Antonio, the future Duke of Cannizzaro, also a Roman Catholic.

Such readiness to subscribe for a good sermon was one sign that the Evangelical movement in the Church of England, associated with men like William Wilberforce, had begun to have an influence in Wimbledon. Evidence of Evangelical practices like family prayers and daily reading of the Bible is hard to find. But the custom of 'dressing the church' at Christmas was started at St Mary's probably at the instigation of Evangelicals in 1815, while their concern for the poor showed in schemes to help those who had suffered badly from the high price of food and fuel in the years after Waterloo. A voluntary subscription in 1818 raised the very large sum of one hundred and seventy pounds to supply the poor with bread, coal and potatoes at a low price. Three years later the first local church charity was launched – a Maternal Society to help 'poor women of good character who had lived in Wimbledon one year'.

The leading Evangelical was not one of the new Curates, but a very formidable American, Mrs Charlotte Marryat. The wife of an influential MP and mother of a large family (including Frederick, a famous novelist), she and her husband bought Wimbledon House Parkside in 1815. When nine years later he dropped dead at his office, she took control and made her large garden one of the finest round London. Then after the Spencers gave up the manor house in 1827, she became the dominating character in the village and its moral conscience.

As mother-in-law of the Vicar, Henry Lindsay, who officially succeeded Randolph in 1819, she had considerable influence in church affairs. In 1840 she even appeared at a meeting of the male-dominated Vestry which was discussing the future of the annual fair in the High Street and helped to secure its suppression on the grounds that it had become disorderly. Instead, she held garden parties in her grounds and raised funds to endow new Almshouses in Camp Road. She also went regularly with other ladies to the Gipsy Camp on the Common and read the Bible to their families. As late as 1910 she was still vividly remembered by old inhabitants who said 'she was as much thought of at Wimbledon as the Queen at Windsor'.

Lindsay was another gentleman parson. Like Randolph, he lived in a house on the Green with his wife and three sons, two of whom later became parsons. He was invited to dine several times at the manor house before the Spencers left and was described by Countess Lavinia as 'our worthy clergyman'. He was certainly a most efficient and conscientious Chairman of Vestry meetings and his signature at the end of the minutes is neat and clear. In 1830 he also became Vicar of Croydon and seems to have spent most of his time there, leaving St Mary's to his Curate, William Edelman. In the early years of Queen Victoria's reign it therefore fell to Edelman to preside at the negotiations for the building of a second new church at Wimbledon.

PART FOUR

The Fourth St Mary's

GILBERT SCOTT'S CHURCH

Debate over a New Church

In May 1839, two years after Victoria had become Queen, the Revd William Edelman presided over a meeting of the Vestry – the rate-payers who controlled local affairs – at the School House in Camp Road. It had been called to discuss the future of the Georgian church, which was already proving too small 'to afford to all thosewho are desirous the opportunity of joining in the service of Almighty God'. Over the past forty years the population of the village had been steadily increasing (from about 1,500 in 1801 to just over 2,600 in 1841) and now a railway link to London had recently been opened at the bottom of the hill. So the church authorities were faced with the problem of either trying to increase the number of 'sittings' in St Mary's or of enlarging the church yet again.

Only thirty-six were at the meeting, but they formed a cross-section of the more prosperous parishioners. Among them were two major-generals (Sir Henry Murray and Adam Hogg who both lived on Southside), a barrister (Alexander Park of Merton Grove), a farmer (Thomas Watney), a doctor (John Sanford), two schoolmasters (Orlando Mayor and William Staton who ran Nelson House School), and several High Street tradesmen (James Holland, a grocer, James Oakman, a butcher, and Daniel Withem, a glazier), as well as the two Churchwardens, James Peache, a wealthy wood merchant who lived at Belvedere House and William Mason, a baker and grandson of the carpenter who had helped to build the Georgian church. General Murray, a dashing cavalry leader at Waterloo and a forthright speaker, at once seized the initiative. He claimed that the church

	VICTORIAN VICARS	
1819-46	Henry Lindsay, MA	Then Rector of Sundridge, Kent
1846-59	Richard Adams, MA	Then Rector of Shere, Surrey
1859-1902	Henry Haygarth, MA	Canon of Rochester

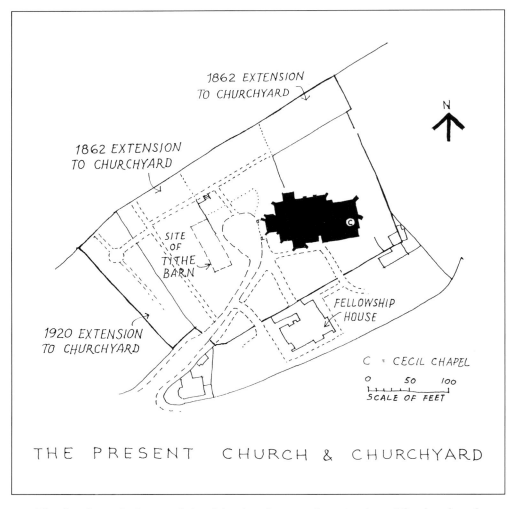

1862 EXTENSION
TO CHURCHYARD

1862 EXTENSION
TO CHURCHYARD

N

SITE
OF
TITHE
BARN

FELLOWSHIP
HOUSE

1920 EXTENSION
TO CHURCHYARD

C = CECIL CHAPEL

0   50   100

SCALE OF FEET

THE PRESENT CHURCH & CHURCHYARD

The plan shows the increased size of the church, successive extensions of the churchyard
and the Fellowship House, built in 1974.

was large enough and to increase its size would be 'a serious expense to no purpose'. He won wide support and it was therefore decided to set up a committee
to help the Churchwardens find the best way to rearrange the seats 'by amicable
arrangement with the present occupiers'. The committee spent months in negotiations, but found the pew-holders not very 'amicable' to their proposals.

So just after Christmas and against the strong opposition of General Murray,
the Vestry decided there was no alternative but to enlarge the church. It therefore
set up a new committee under Edelman to decide how best to carry this out;

among its members was an architect, John Griffith, who promptly offered to submit his own plan free. His fellow members, however, preferred to commission 'an eminent London Surveyor', David Roper, who was asked to design a church with 400 'extra sittings'. His first plan proved 'unequal to the increased accommodation' and the committee discussed the possibility of building an entirely new church on a new site, perhaps on the Common. The discussion was swiftly ended by Mr Roper who now produced three plans, one of which the committee thought 'most eligible', perhaps because it would cost less than £1,400, even though it only provided 140 extra sittings.

For almost a year nothing seems to have happened. Then in February 1841 Roper was asked to have an amended plan ready in a month's time 'for carrying out the work'. He produced a new design providing more than double the extra sittings (300), at slightly less than double the cost (£2,700). Still the committee were not satisfied. They decided 400 extra sittings were essential since 300 of them were needed as 'free seats' for the use of poor parishioners. Roper seems to have been unwilling to adapt his plans any more. So he was paid his fee, only £85, and informed that the committee could not recommend any of his designs.

Two years had now gone by and the problem of extra seats appeared no nearer solution. Yet in the next two months it was solved to the satisfaction of almost everyone – except General Murray. In May 1841 the committee decided to ask a thirty-year-old architect living in Vauxhall, George Gilbert Scott, and his partner, William Moffat, to produce a suitable plan. The resulting designs greatly impressed them, combining 'much architectural beauty with the requisite increase in church accommodation' and providing 'due regard for God's honour and glory'. The building would cost about £4,000 (double the Georgian church), but seemed to provide the extra 400 sittings.

The committee were delighted and in July strongly recommended that the plans be accepted. A contract was drawn up under which the new nave was to be covered by 1 December 1841, while the entire work was to be completed by 1 June the following year. Half the money was to be raised by voluntary subscription (with James Peache promptly giving £100 and Alexander Park £50); the rest was to be borrowed on the security of the Church Rate. Here again Mr Peache helped by loaning the whole £2000 and agreeing to be paid back at only £100 a year. Work on the church could start at once.

George Gilbert Scott

St Mary's Wimbledon is just one of the five hundred or more churches that Scott built or restored in a long life. In addition he designed some of the most famous Victorian buildings in London, including the Albert Memorial, the Foreign Office and St Pancras Hotel. His work was on such a scale that, according to Sir Kenneth Clark, 'it must have changed the appearance of England considerably'.

In 1841 Scott was only beginning to make his name. Seven years earlier he had gone into partnership with William Moffat, originally his clerk of the works. They quickly built up a successful practice by what Scott described as 'dirty, disagreeable work', building Workhouses for the new Poor Law Unions. They then began to design churches, mostly 'small commissions of little importance', among them St Peter's, Norbiton.

1841 in fact was a crucial year for Scott. He met the architect-apostle of the Gothic Revival, Augustus Welby Pugin, and promptly became an enthusiast for Gothic architecture. His early churches, however, were strongly criticised by Benjamin Webb, secretary of the Cambridge Camden Society, founded only two years before to stimulate interest in the principles of true (i.e. Gothic) architecture. Scott accepted many of the criticisms and began to design churches in accordance with the 'ideal' Decorated style of the fourteenth century, with great stress on the altar and chancel, a much lower pulpit with a reading-desk or lectern (on opposite sides of the chancel arch) and open seats all facing east instead of the old box-pews.

In the next few years Scott designed his first successful Gothic buildings, including the Martyrs' Memorial Oxford and St Giles Church, Camberwell. In his 'Recollections' of the period around 1840, however, he referred with contempt to 'the cheap church mania' when buildings were put up at 'so many shillings a sitting', most 'begalleried to the very eyes', with plaster used for internal fittings, even for pillars. He regarded his work on such churches as 'days of abject degradation' and often wished that the buildings had been burnt down. He never mentioned St Mary's by name among them, but there can be little doubt from his remarks on 'the cheap church mania' that he was not very proud of it.

Building the Church

Not long after Scott started work on the church, General Murray left for a new appointment in Ireland. He sent a parting message to his colleagues on the Vestry - 'Keep strictly within the limits of the money provided and ensure there is no

(*left*) James Courthope Peache (1781-1858), Churchwarden in 1838-39, 1843-44 and 1856, as well as a great benefactor to the church. (*right*) Sir George Gilbert Scott (1811-1878), the architect of the fourth St Mary's.

delay in the opening of the church'. Both points were to be forgotten in the next two years, perhaps because of one of the last motions he proposed in the Vestry: that, as with the Georgian church, when allocating the work preference should be given to Wimbledon tradesmen.

In July 1841, therefore, the work was put out to tender to local builders. Two were not interested. The others formed two combines. One from the High Street (Benjamin Burt and Daniel Mason) sent in an estimate totalling £4,128, but the second from Church Road (William Parsons with two carpenters, William Finch and James Goswell) undercut them with a tender of £3,839, which naturally was accepted.

Work started in August and services had to stop at St Mary's. Edward Eades, a High Street grocer, offered the use of his large thatched barn near the Dog and Fox. It was gratefully accepted, but needed a lot of modification before it

The first photograph taken of St Mary's – in 1862. The clock was not then installed on the tower, while the tithe barn on the left was dismantled shortly afterwards so that the churchyard could be extended.

could be used by a congregation of about five hundred. The outside had to be repaired and repainted. Mats, seats and hat-pegs had to be put in, along with two hot-air stoves, an organ and a bell. John Dossett, the official rat-catcher, was asked to 'search for rats' and charged four shillings for 'destroying a rat or rates [sic]' in the barn. Finally David Penner, one of the local Constables, was paid two guineas for 'attending and keeping order in the stable yard and in the Dog and Fox Alley on Sundays while Divine Service was held in the barn'.

Meanwhile, Scott and Moffat were supervising Parsons and his workmen. First they pulled down the Georgian entrance apse with the tower and spire. Then they lengthened the nave thirty-five feet to the west and built a new tower and steeple, 196 feet high, with 'a proper lightning conductor' on top. They kept the rest of the Georgian nave, but covered both old and new brick with knapped flints to make the whole look of one period. They supported the extra weight of the walls and of a fine hammer-beam roof by adding buttresses between the windows, which were enlarged and given Perpendicular tracery. The main entrance was now at the west end, but there was also a porch on the south side.

If the outside of the church seemed Gothic, the interior of the nave was still Georgian, though with Gothic detail. New galleries were put in for wealthy parishioners. As in the Georgian church, they were supported by cast iron girders covered with plaster to look like stone pillars. The Gothic chancel had to be left untouched with its Georgian pews and high pulpit. But all the arches were now pointed and new low pews were put in the nave. In addition, a new organ, the gift of the very generous James Peache, was installed as the old one was 'insufficient and not worth repairing', and a 'handsome' royal coat of arms, made of artificial stone and presented by Mrs Marryat, was placed above the chancel arch.

The new church opened in March 1843, nine months later than promised. It seems never to have provided the extra 400 sittings expected (with a lot of children present, 1,000 could be squeezed in, but there is no record of 1,100 being seated and today 800 is the comfortable maximum, only 100 more than in the Georgian church). Scott did, however, build the church within the promised budget. As Jack Harvey remarked in his *Short History*: 'What he achieved for £4,000 (even allowing for the greater value of money in those days) is truly remarkable.' There is, however, one qualification: while Scott and Moffat were promptly paid their fee of £750, the unfortunate Parsons and his two associates had to wait for five years for their final £800. In 1845 they complained to the

Vestry, who agreed that it was 'a subject of regret' that 'industrious tradesmen' should suffer 'such inconvenience' because not everyone who had promised a subscription had actually sent the money. So, having pledged that no more than £2,000 would be raised by a compulsory Church Rate, the Vestry tried to get parishioners to make voluntary contributions, but no-one seemed ready to give any more. In the end the debt was paid in April 1848 by James Peache and two of the Churchwardens at the time of the rebuilding, William Brown and Daniel Withem.

Even after the reconsecration, the church was not finished. In 1844 three hot-air stoves were installed, but they produced problems with the ventilation. Another committee was set up to deal with this. In the end it recommended opening windows at the east end, but these promptly led to complaints of draughts. Then in 1849 the roof needed repair. In 1877 the tower was completed with a large clock presented by the publisher, John Murray of Newstead House, and a third bell was added to the two already given ten years earlier by James Wilson of Cambridge House, Church Road. Along with the three older bells, they provided 'chimes every Sunday morning'.

By then the chancel had been redesigned to fit in with the nave. In 1860 the Ecclesiastical Commissioners allowed their architect Ewan Christian to remove the Georgian additions – the two large galleried pews and the false plaster roof. Old oak rafters were revealed and decorated very simply. New benches were put in on each side, an arch made into the Cecil Chapel and a vestry built between the chapel and the end of the south aisle (where the Warrior Chapel is today). The old communion table seems to have been retained, but it was now given a reredos, 'a handsome frame made of oak', instead of the traditional black board with the Ten Commandments on it. Above was a new east window commemorating James Peache, who had died in 1858, 'one of the most respected members' of the congregation.

At last Wimbledon had a worthy parish church. Sir Thomas Jackson, a leading local architect who designed the Warrior Chapel, dismissed it as 'respectable for its date, but monotonous and uninteresting'. Sir John Betjeman did not think it worthy of inclusion in any of his books on parish churches. Jack Harvey, was kinder in his judgement: 'Working within the confines imposed on him, Scott left us a noble building, which in many respects bears the hallmarks of genius.' Many of the congregation at St Mary's now seem to agree with this view; their main criticism is of Scott's very uncomfortable pews.

A drawing made by W.J. Allen about 1870 showing the church from the drive leading to the Manor House with the gate at Stag Lodge to the left. The drive was soon to become Arthur Road. The trees in the centre cover the site of Fellowship House.

A SEATING PLAN FOR THE NEW CHURCH

In the Wimbledon Society Museum there is a rather battered Vestry Notebook simply headed 'Wimbledon', but clearly made in the 1840s and early 1850s. It contains a great variety of information, much of it connected with the newly-rebuilt church. There are donation and subscription lists, records of the monuments in the church and of the graves in the churchyard, exact drawings of the memorial windows, an outline sketch of the Cecil Chapel – and a detailed plan of the seating arrangements in the nave.

The plan is headed 'Pews and Sittings 1845'. In fact it must have been made two years earlier for the reopening of the church as the Vicar's pew is occupied by the Curate-in-charge, the Revd William Edelman. In November 1843 he was appointed Vicar of Merton and his place at St Mary's was taken by the Revd Richard Adams.

The plan illustrates very clearly the social distinctions in early Victorian Wimbledon. The 'best seats' in the church were then in the galleries (in 1790 their annual rent was fixed at three guineas for the front row, two for the second, and one and a half for the third). So there sat all the important landowners with their families. Among them were: James Peache (Belvedere House), Mrs Marryat (Wimbledon House, Parkside), Major Oliphant (Lingfield House), General Murray (Wimbledon Lodge), Miss Wright and General Hogg (two unnamed houses that are now called Southside House), Edward Holroyd (Gothic Lodge), William Brown

(Woodhayes), William Leake (Mount Ararat), the Earl of Cottenham (Prospect Place), Sir Thomas Shaw-Lefevre (Westside House), Arthur Eden (Cannizaro) and Alexander Park (Merton Grove). Behind them (and in the aisles below) sat their 'men servants' – but there seems to have been no place for the 'females'. At the western end were the children from the National School on the Common.

Down below in the nave were 'pews and sittings' which since 1790 could be rented for one and a half guineas a year. They were occupied by farmers, like Thomas Watney and John Caswell, and by virtually all the tradesmen in the High Street: two grocers – Edward Eades and Thomas Mason; two butchers – James Oakman and Michael Ogden; a baker – William Mason; a tailor – Richard Roffey; a glazier – Daniel Withem; and a 'victualler' – William Packer at the Dog and Fox. There were also the village's first surgeon – Thomas Tapley; the first vet – John Hayter; and the first estate agent (and also a builder) – Daniel Mason. Two other interesting seat-holders were William Parsons, the builder of the nave, and James Paxton, a market gardener and brother of the creator of the Crystal Palace.

Behind all these local dignatories, along with the boys of Nelson House School were the 'free seats' for ordinary Wimbledonians. With a population of over 2,600 and room in the church for 1,000 at most, a lot of them could never have been fitted in – even if they had wanted to attend morning service. The old, however, were cared for with seats under the pulpit for 'the Aged Men' and by the reading desk for 'the Aged Women'.

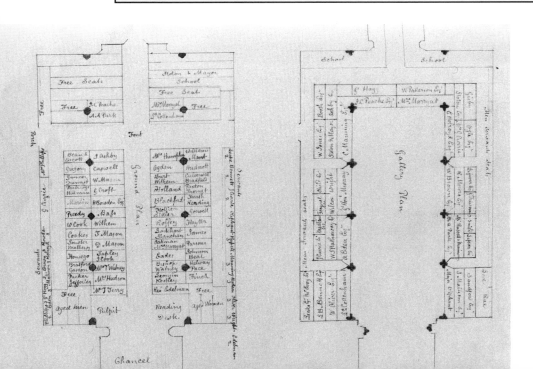

The seating plan of the Fourth St Mary's in 1843.

THE VICTORIAN TRANSFORMATION OF THE PARISH

Growth of New Wimbledon

The completion of the fourth St Mary's in 1860 came just a year after an event of even greater significance in the long history of the parish: the consecration of Christ Church in Cottenham Park as a chapel-of-ease. Ever since late Saxon times there had been only one church in Wimbledon and on Sundays everyone in the village had been expected to attend it. From now onwards churches and chapels, not merely of the Established Church, but of all denominations were built so regularly that by 1914 instead of one church there were twenty-three in the borough.

This great increase was not the result of a new fervour for religion sweeping the area. In 1851 when an official religious census was taken, only a third of the villagers were present at morning service in St Mary's. Just over fifty years later when an unofficial census was printed in *The Daily News*, the proportion of the population in churches all over Wimbledon was almost exactly the same, though by now they numbered nearly 14,000 instead of about 750.

These figures in fact registered the transformation that had taken place in those fifty years. In 1851 the population of the village had been just under 2,700. By 1901 there were over 41,000 people living in what had become a suburb of London. As soon as Wimbledon had been made a junction for trains going to Kingston, Croydon and Epsom, families had started flocking in from all over the country – the poorer ones to find work, the middle-class to buy large new houses in almost country surroundings. The poorer families had settled mostly near the station on either side of the Broadway. The middle-class homes had rather been up the hill, especially in the new estates developed in Wimbledon Park and Cottenham Park.

Their arrival posed the Vicar at St Mary's with problems that none of his predecessors had ever had to face. The sheer number of people meant that the fourth parish church was too small almost before it was finished and that the radical idea put forward in 1841 for a totally new church on a new site would have to be reconsidered. Then the fact that a large proportion of the newcomers were relatively poor and liable to be thrown out of work during hard winters or slumps in trade made the parson feel duty-bound to extend the charitable organisations that had started in a small way in the 1820s. Finally, the settling in the parish of so many well-educated, highly responsible professional men was a new challenge to the clergy's leadership. The Spencers had left the area for good in 1827; few other noble families remained; and Mrs Marryat had died in 1854. From now on it was the barristers, the doctors, the civil engineers and the successful businessmen who would have to be asked for help in promoting the work of the church.

These men were mostly members of the Church of England. But their views on religion and above all on the type of service needed on Sundays did not necessarily coincide with those of the Vicar. Since the 1830s controversy had been raging over the demands of the Tractarians on the one hand for greater stress on the Sacraments and for brighter services, and of the Evangelicals on the other for great emphasis on the Bible and for more heart-felt sermons. There was also controversy over the payment for seats in church. Some laymen argued that it was this system of pew rents that kept 'working people' away as it 'treated them as strangers in the House of God'.

If working-class families went to church, they were now more likely to go to one of the new Nonconformist meeting-places. Wimbledon's first, described as

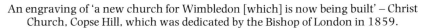

An engraving of 'a new church for Wimbledon [which] is now being built' – Christ Church, Copse Hill, which was dedicated by the Bishop of London in 1859.

'a very small Dissenting Chapel', had been set up just off the High Street by a Congregational minister in the 1840s. Sixty years later large churches had been built by the Methodists, Presbyterians and Baptists, as well as the Congregationalists, and their joint congregations were slightly larger than those attending the Anglican churches. On top of that, Roman Catholics had returned to an area once described as 'a stronghold of Protestantism' and already had big attendances at their fine new church on Edge Hill.

The problems faced by religion in the second half of the nineteenth century were daunting. But they came at a time when politically Britain was regarded as the greatest Power in the world. The prosperity of her trade and industry was shown in the Great Exhibition of 1851. Her superior attitude to foreigners was personified by Lord Palmerston, Prime Minister at the end of the Crimean War (1854-56). Her naval prestige enabled her to build a world-wide Empire, above all in India over which the Tory Prime Minister Disraeli declared the Queen Empress in 1876. And it was Victoria's Golden and Diamond Jubilees in 1887 and 1897 which enabled the country to end the century in a haze of glory. A very different outlook on Britain's position was symbolised by a third Prime Minister, the Liberal Mr Gladstone. His life was dedicated to reform, above all of Britain's troubled relations with Ireland, and he won widespread support.

Revd Henry Haygarth

The task of guiding the parish in such a fast-changing era fell in 1859 to a 38-year-old Vicar, the Revd Henry Haygarth. His ancestors came from Yorkshire, though his parents had settled in the South. His older brother, a colonel in the army, fought in the Crimea. A younger brother, Arthur, was a keen cricketer and compiled *Scores and Biographies*, an essential reference book for matches before 1864 when *Wisden* started. Henry was educated at Eton and Magdalen College, Oxford, but did not consider entering the Church until he had spent eight years working in Australia and writing a book on his experiences. Ordained in 1853 at the age of thirty-two, he worked for six years as a Curate in Essex before being appointed Vicar of Wimbledon shortly after his marriage.

He needed all his experience of life for the demanding new job. But he did have one advantage: his predecessor, the Revd Richard Adams, Vicar for the previous thirteen years (1846-59), had already suggested solutions to the problems. Adams had presided over the building of Christ Church, which aimed to serve the new middle-class residents of Cottenham Park. He had also sent one of the

(*above, left*) Revd Richard Adams (1802-1875). He was Vicar of Wimbledon from 1846 to 1859, and then became Rector of Shere in Surrey. (*above right*) Revd William Bartlett (1832-1895). He was a Curate under Haygarth from 1860 to 1868, when he became Vicar of Wisborough Green, Sussex. (*right*) Canon Henry Haygarth (1821-1902). This is the only known photograph of the long-serving Vicar.

first two assistant Curates at St Mary's to found a mission centre off the Broadway to serve the poorer families of New Wimbledon, and had encouraged the start of a Loan Blanket Society to help the poor during the winter. The controversy over services he had ignored by simply following a strongly Evangelical line. The reaction of two of his leading parishioners, Thomas Hughes, author of *Tom Brown's Schooldays*, and J.M. Ludlow, a barrister (both Christian Socialists), was significant. They accused Adams of being 'too fond of hell-fire sermons' and organised their own services in the library at the Firs, the house their families shared in Copse Hill.

Haygarth was a very different character from Adams. He was a very conservative, Low Church Anglican who hated making changes or coming to firm decisions. One of his parishioners described him as 'a survival from the past'. He wore the clerical dress of the early years of the century and always preached in a black gown, refusing to put on one of the new surplices. In the pulpit he was a striking figure with 'his bright, bird-like eyes, aristocratic face, long silvery hair and white choker'. He seemed 'very eccentric, yet was loved by the parish'.

The reason for this affection is clear from the very thorough *Parish Reports* that Haygarth produced year after year from 1860 until just before his death in 1902. Each started with an 'address', first to 'my Christian friends', later to 'my dear parishioners', explaining the general state of the parish. Then followed long lists of good causes – schools, charities, new churches – with the names of contributors, along with the money given for special collections and at the end the total amount contributed for the use of the church. It was very impressive, justifying the Vicar's opening comments in 1861: 'I feel I have much to be thankful for'. Yet every so often his worries got the better of him. In 1872 he alluded to 'many appeals made in vain, letters to which no response has been given and many a chilling silence' with 'the chief burden borne by comparatively few'. Yet his main message is one of hope and of trust in the Lord: 'There has been much spiritual growth in the past year [1875-76] and much visible good. We work steadily and hopefully on, praying much ourselves and desiring your prayers for us, thanking God for the help he has given us.'

Henry Haygarth clearly lived for his parish. He faced 'cheerfully the constant demands upon our time and money' and aimed 'to promote the spiritual and temporal welfare of the community'. He rarely left Wimbledon except for a holiday in August; he loved books, but had little time for reading; he was quite an artist, but only took out his sketch-book when on holiday. His longest-serving Curate, the Revd C.C. Chamberlain (1874-97) described him as 'kindly, open, genuine and sincere'. His natural dislike of change was tempered by his wide range of interests and concerns. He was determined that the new residents of Wimbledon must be provided with churches, help in times of trouble and a means of Christian education. Hence, partly out of his own pocket, he helped to finance the building of four new Anglican churches: Holy Trinity, St John's, St Mark's and All Saints. He encouraged the many societies set up by the Church to help the poor in New Wimbledon. To preserve the parish from 'God-less' Board Schools he raised a great deal of money (£4,000 of it his own) to build more parochial schools with places for over four thousand children. And every Monday he personally gave religious instruction at the National School in Camp Road. Outside St Mary's his most important work, he felt, was his campaign for temperance reform.'The struggle against the demon drink', as he called it in one *Report*, occupied a lot of his time from 1868. He wrote pamphlets, organised meetings and promoted Coffee Taverns to keep working-men from the pubs.

In carrying on all these many works, Haygarth had to rely heavily on others, above all his Curates and Churchwardens. Starting with two Curates in 1859, he was working with six by the time of his death. Perhaps the one who had the most lasting effect was William Bartlett who founded Holy Trinity church

ANGLICAN INSTITUTIONS TO HELP THE POOR	
1821 Maternal Society	To help 'poor women of good character'
1841 Provident Medical Dispensary	To provide 'gratuitous medical assistance and medicines'
1844 Friendly Society	For mutual relief in sickness, old age, death
1858 Loan Blanket Society	For use of poor, especially sick, during winter
1859 Clothing, Bedding and Fuel Club	To help 'responsible labourers and their families'
District Visitors	To find by 'kind and inoffensive enquiry' the needs of 'the deserving poor'
Penny Bank	To help the poor to save
1884 Emigration Society	To help young unemployed get to Canada

(*left*) Keziah Peache (?-1899), only daughter of James Peache and organist at St Mary's from 1854 to 1869. (*right*) Henry C. Forde (1827-1897), Churchwarden at St Mary's from 1885 to 1894. His widow gave the brass lectern in his memory.

and wrote the first history of Wimbledon in 1865. But without 'lay help, well selected and well sustained', Haygarth knew he could not manage 'this increasing parish'. Among the helpers were many ladies, especially the District Visitors, the Sunday School teachers and the amazing Keziah Peache, the only daughter of James Peache of Belvedere House, who played the organ in St Mary's for fifteen years and devoted her considerable fortune to good works. It was, however, to the Churchwardens that the Vicar mainly turned for advice and support, men like George Pollock (1860-66) a distinguished lawyer, Henry Forde (1885-94) a civil engineer commemorated by the eagle lectern in St Mary's, and John Partridge (1874-96) on whose tombstone in the churchyard there is the inscription: 'A faithful Churchwarden to this parish for twenty-four years' (in fact twenty-three), a record never likely to be beaten.

The work of all these very different people had as its focus not merely the church, but Wimbledon's first Vicarage (now flats known as Steeple Court, just to the west of the Old Rectory). Haygarth was wealthy enough to be able to buy

Two views of Haygarth's St Mary's taken about 1900. They show the high wooden pulpit from which he preached his long sermons, the desk opposite from which he conducted the rest of the service and the newly-installed lectern. At the east end of the chancel the altar is not yet raised. Above it are the new stained glass windows, a memorial to James Peache.

the land from the Ecclesiastical Commissioners, build a large house, staff it with six servants and lay out a fine garden, full of his favourite roses – and his hens. He used it as a parish centre for his Curates (who all lived in rooms elsewhere) and as a home where he and his wife entertained friends and parishioners. The death of his wife in 1876 was 'an irreparable loss' according to Chamberlain. 'I was not equal to much during part of the autumn,' Haygarth later wrote, 'though I found in the work itself some slight relief in the day of affliction.' Five years later his only son died on the eve of marriage. The Vicar was devastated, yet met the second blow 'with patient resignation'. He continued working and carrying on 'a most voluminous correspondence' almost to the day of his death.

Controversy over Services

On one matter Haygarth provoked bitter controversy, the services at St Mary's. During his forty-two years as Vicar, they hardly changed: Morning Service with a long sermon every Sunday at 11 am and Evensong with another sermon at 3.30 pm (moved to 6.30 pm after the church was lit by gas in 1863). Communion was only celebrated after Mattins on the first Sunday of every month and on the great feasts of Easter, Whitsun, Trinity and Christmas, but 'at the request of some parishioners', in 1868 an 8 am Communion Service was held on the third Sunday of the month.

Haygarth was well pleased with attendances. In 1862 he told his Bishop (now the Bishop of London) that 'except for the working-men' a fair proportion of the population went to church, that there were about 900 at Morning Service and 500 at Evensong, that Communicants on the first Sundays numbered about 100 and were increasing, and that 'the tone' of the congregation was 'earnest and devout'. Thirty years later he described the parishioners as 'very attentive and devout in church', though he was sad that 'some families' persistently came late.

Some of the congregation were not so happy. They found the services dull and old-fashioned, based on a forty-minute sermon which was 'rambling and full of quotations from obscure theologians'. They knew from his first *Report* of 1860 that their Vicar regarded good music and congregational singing as playing 'an important part in Divine Service'. But they were upset by his ban on the use of the newly-published *Hymns, Ancient and Modern*, which was Tractarian in inspiration. Not until 1881 'in compliance with the wishes of some of my parishioners' were sixty hymns, 'carefully chosen and set to pleasing tunes' by the organist, added to the old dreary hymnal.

As a result, from the start of his ministry, Haygarth provoked a lot of strong criticism from the two wings of the church, the Evangelicals and the Tractarians. The Evangelicals were bitterly disappointed that he had abandoned the more fervent type of service used in St Mary's under Adams in the 1850s. They started holding meetings in private houses to pray and read the Bible. Then in 1861 (supposedly led by five 'holy Colonels') they seceded from the parish church, put up an iron chapel at the top of Grosvenor Hill and held their own services. Their support grew. In 1888 they built a permanent church on the Ridgway, Emmanuel, and by the time of Haygarth's death their congregation was as large as that at St Mary's.

The Tractarians were not so numerous, nor so single-minded, but they were just as critical of the services. In 1871 they sent Haygarth a 'memorandum' signed by fifty-two 'heads of families' expressing 'considerable dissatisfaction' with 'the lugubrious and unattractive' services which had led many to stop going to St Mary's on Sunday. They asked for services which would 'express their reverential and devotional feelings' – a weekly celebration of Communion and a Choral Service with good music and a well-trained surpliced choir singing from the chancel. If the Vicar would not allow such services in one of the churches in the parish, they asked leave to build a separate church (as the Evangelicals had done) or to use the school chapel at Eagle House.

Haygarth, supported by his Churchwardens and his Bishop, refused any concession as a matter of conscience. He listened patiently to all requests for change, but was convinced that he was right to insist on all churches in the parish keeping uniform services. 'There are many shades of opinion in our Church,' he wrote in the 1861 *Report*, 'but we must try to keep unity of the spirit in the bond of peace.' In the face of some very strong criticism, 'he never', according to Chamberlain, 'answered hard words with hard words.'

Even his strongest opponents realised that Haygarth was 'actuated by the highest motives' and found it impossible to dislike him. They were pleased when in 1868 he was officially made a Vicar instead of being merely a Perpetual Curate. They were delighted when ten years later he was made one of the first Canons of the new diocese of Rochester (to which Wimbledon had just been transferred despite Haygarth's opposition as he felt 'we have no connection with Rochester'). They were saddened when news spread of his sudden death.

Canon Haygarth died from pneumonia at the Vicarage on the last day of 1902. He was eighty-one and had been in failing health. But he had taken Morning

Service on Christmas Day and his death came as a shock. The editor of *The Wimbledon News* expressed the feelings of many when he wrote: 'The Vicar had been identified with the parish for so long that it is difficult to imagine Wimbledon without his kindly presence.' At his funeral St Mary's was packed. The Bishops of Rochester and Southwark were present along with four Nonconformist ministers and a Guard of Honour from the Surrey Volunteers (as Haygarth had been their Honorary Chaplain). Many shops were shut and the blinds of private houses drawn as a mark of respect. Memorial services were held at the other churches in the parish. At one, a parson who had known him well declared that the secret of his success lay in one factor above all: 'He was a man of prayer'. Later, Chamberlain, his ex-Curate, summed him up as 'a good, if not a great man'. It was for such reasons that he was able to provide a vital stabilising influence that enabled St Mary's to flourish during a period of bewildering change.

The memorial to Canon Haygarth, placed on the north wall of the chancel three years after his death.

NEW ANGLICAN CHURCHES IN WIMBLEDON

1859	Christ Church, Copse Hill	1961	Made separate parish
1862	Holy Trinity, Broadway	1872	Made separate parish
1875	St John's, Spencer Hill*		
1880	St Mark's, Hill Road*		
1888	Emmanuel, Ridgway		Extra-parochial
1892	All Saints, Haydons Road		Part of Holy Trinity parish
1909	St Mathew's, Durham Road*		
	St Luke's, Wimbledon Park	1910	Made separate parish
	St Andrew's, South Wimbledon	1910	Made separate parish
1911	St Peter's, near Haydons Road	1912	Made separate parish

**still part of the parish of Wimbledon*

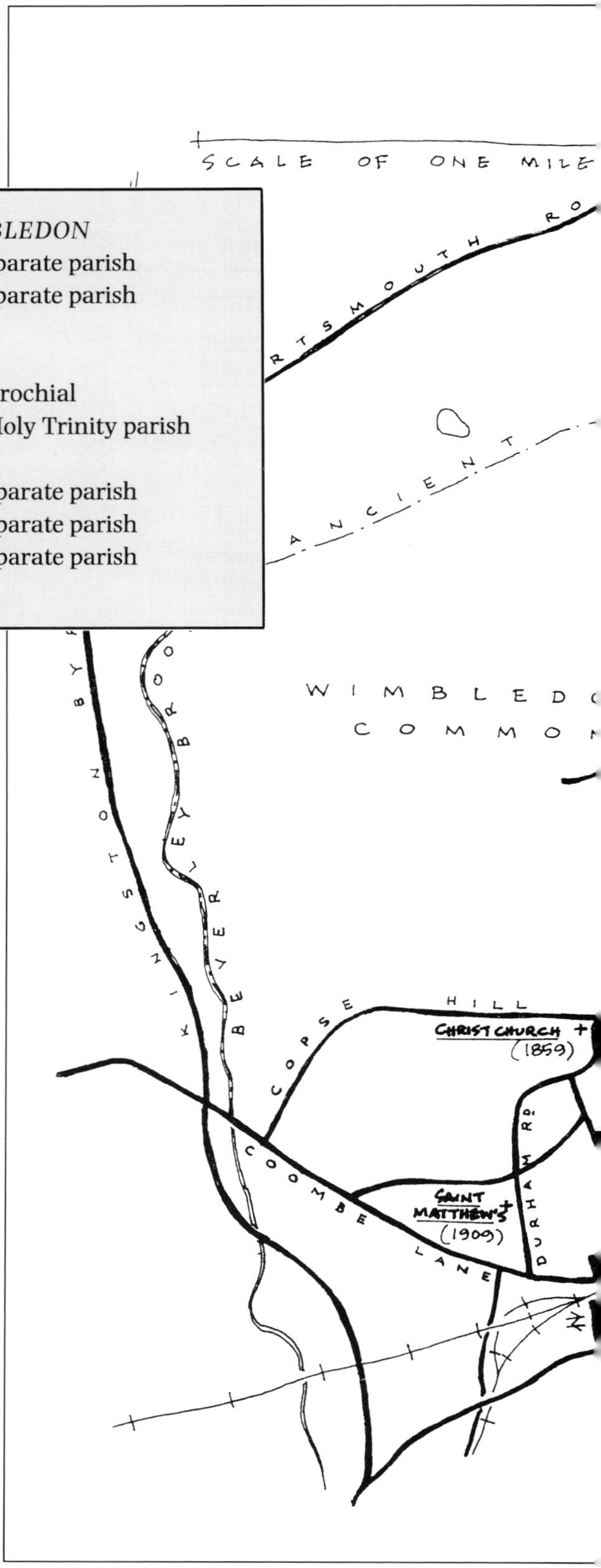
SCALE OF ONE MILE
RTSMOUTH RO
ANCIENT
WIMBLEDO
COMMO
KINGSTON BY
BEVERLEY BROOK
COPSE HILL
CHRIST CHURCH
(1859)
SAINT MATTHEW'S
(1909)
COOMBE LANE
DURHAM RD

Ten new Anglican churches were built in just over fifty years, between 1859 and 1911, a real achievement. They covered the entire built-up area of the new suburb and led to the creation of five new parishes.

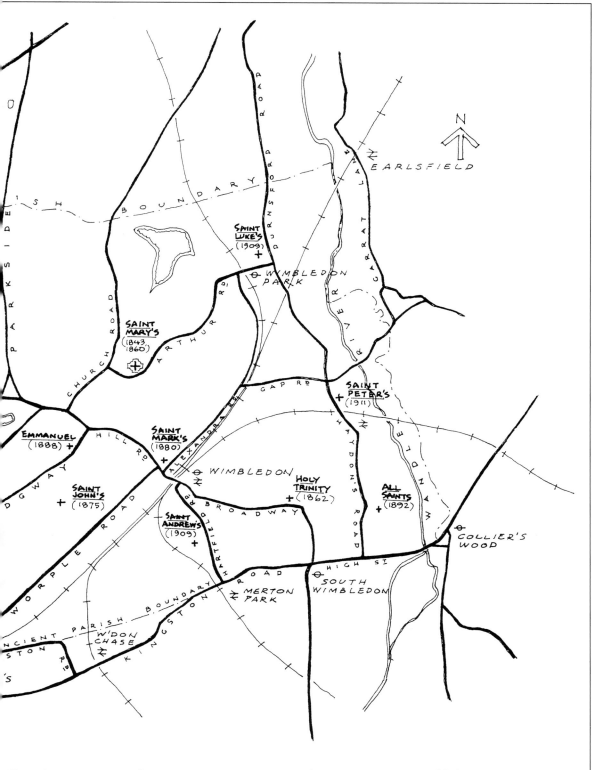

EW ANGLICAN CHURCHES IN WIMBLEDON SINCE 1840

St Mary's from the churchyard gates.

THE CHURCH IN TWO WORLD WARS

Services at St Mary's

The forty-two years that Canon Haygarth spent at St Mary's witnessed a complete transformation of the parish. Over the next forty-two years (1903-45) he had four successors:

    1903-18   Canon James Bell, MA
    1918-30   Canon Horace Monroe, MA
    1930-32   The Revd Edward Tupper, MA
    1932-45   Canon Arthur Phelips, MA.

They had to face changes that were at least as challenging. These ranged from two world wars and the slump of the 1930s to the invention of the aeroplane and the founding of the BBC. There were also major developments in the Church of England: a big decline in support especially among the middle-class in the South-East, general recognition that communion was as least as important as the sermon, and a slow improvement in relations between the Churches.

St Mary's was affected by most of these developments. But there seems to have

been no decline in attendance at Sunday services and there was a considerable increase in the number going to communion, especially at Easter.

Much of the credit for this 'deepening of spiritual life' must go to Haygarth's immediate successor, the Revd James Allen Bell (whose eldest son later became Bishop of Chichester). According to *The Church Times* of 1903, his new parish 'had been in a deplorable state as the dreariest of dreary Protestantism had failed to

Canon James Allen Bell (*c* 1856-1934), Vicar of Wimbledon from 1903 to 1918. On retirement he became Canon Residentiary of Norwich Cathedral.

attract the people'. Bell certainly 'woke things up'. He introduced a Communion Service every Sunday morning at eight and made the services as a whole 'much brighter'. For this he was bitterly attacked in the *Wimbledon News* for 'altering the whole character of church services' and especially for making the evening service choral. He was even denounced by the Protestant Alliance as 'working for the Church of Rome'.

In fact, apart from the extra communion, his services and those of his three successors were very similar to Haygarth's. The sermons were almost certainly better, but the main Sunday services were still Mattins at 11 am and Evensong at 6.30 or 7 pm. The church itself remained 'not very warm and rather dark'. One small boy remembered it in the years just before 1914 as 'filled with a musty smell and a vast amount of dark brown wood-work'. He recalled one relic of

(*opposite*) The interior of St Mary's about 1914 before the Warrior Chapel was built. The photograph shows the new stone pulpit erected in 1912, the Perry monument at the end of the south aisle and the electric lights installed in 1902. (*below*) Canon Bell and his nine assistant Curates, 1908-1910. The Curates served five churches in Wimbledon. Most lived in a large Clergy House in the Ridgway (almost opposite Rydons) and continued their training under an experienced Principal.

Haygarth's time – a pew opener: 'an old lady in a bonnet who ushered in families to their pews; she could be most unpleasant to the most innocent of gate-crashers.'

St Mary's assumed its present appearance in the years immediately before and after the First World War. In 1907 the Chancel was reorganised with a new 'altar table' (later raised up four steps), a new oak screen beside the Cecil Chapel and new stalls in place of the old pews. Five years later a new stone pulpit, designed by Geoffrey Pinkerton, was erected in memory of Mrs Boustead, whose family used to live at Cannizaro (in 1920 it was moved from the south to the north side of the chancel arch). A new 'heating apparatus' was also installed. It was said to have been needed as some of the congregation 'complain of suffocation' because they were too near the stove; others meanwhile were shivering as they had 'to sit in the cold draught'.

In 1920 the biggest addition to the church for nearly eighty years was dedicated – the Warrior Chapel. Designed by Sir Thomas Jackson, a distinguished architect

Sir Thomas Jackson (1835-1924), architect of the Warrior Chapel, which can be seen on the facing page.

(*above*) The chancel before the First World War, with the old pews still in place and a curtain across the Cecil Chapel, then used as a Vestry. (*right*) The Chancel in 1921 after the Warrior Chapel had been built, with the open latticework screen, new stalls and the altar raised.

who lived at Eagle House, it was a memorial to Wimbledonians killed in the recent war. It was built on the site of the old vestry, so a new vestry and choir room had to be added to the south side of the church (and in 1950 a special clergy vestry as well).

Finally, just before the start of the Second World War a new baptistery, designed by W.H. Randoll Blacking, was built in memory of the developer of Wimbledon Park, John Augustus Beaumont, and paid for by his daughter, Lady Lane. It was the brain-child of one of the Churchwardens, A.J. Castle, who wanted that corner of the church to have 'a less cramped appearance' and to allow plenty of room for baptisms. He is said to have 'practically carried it through himself' and in the process so wore himself out that he died a year later.

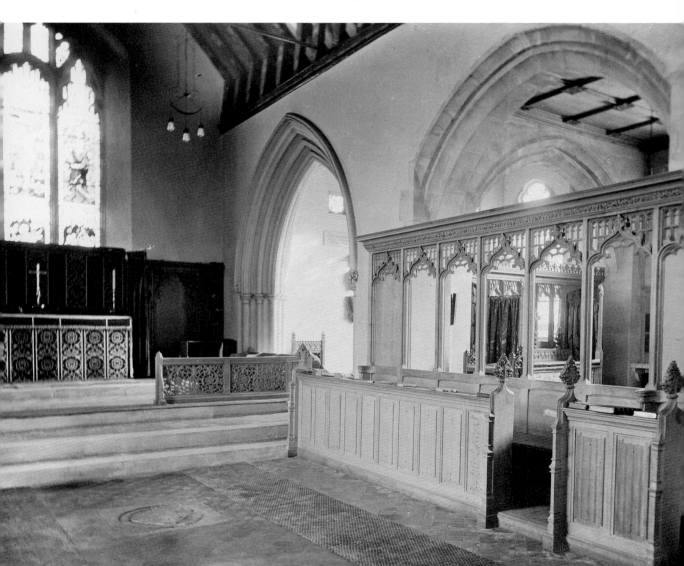

(*above*) The oak tester above the altar, with panelling on either side, put up in 1935 as a memorial to Canon and Mrs Monroe. (*right*) Canon Horace Monroe (*c* 1870-1933), Vicar of Wimbledon from 1918 to 1930. On retirement he became Sub-Dean of Southwark Cathedral.

Canon Horace Monroe and George Berry

The only Vicar apart from Canon Haygarth to have been honoured by a memorial inside the church is Canon Horace Monroe (1918-30). Designed by Mr Downing, the memorial consists of an oak tester above the altar and panelling and shields on either side. It was erected shortly after the Canon's sad death in 1933 during a voyage to America. His obituaries described him as 'a most loved and successful Vicar' and 'an active and genial personality'. He was a small man with a strong Irish accent, noted for his sermons, his lively children's services, his 'warmth and humanity' and for going round the parish in top hat and frock coat.

He succeeded the popular, though controversial Canon Bell in the final months of the First World War. His appointment was only announced after the Dean of Worcester had made enquiries about the kind of Vicar the parish wanted. He was told: 'Not a party man, but one able to sympathise with points of view not his own.'

Monroe certainly lived up to expectations. During the long, controversial debate in 1928 over the revision of the Prayer Book, he managed to keep the parish 'free of bitterness'. He was said to be 'to the front in every good cause – the hospitals, the Guild of Social Welfare, the League of Nations Union, the Christian Social Council'. He held garden parties at the Vicarage and started a St Mary's Society 'to bring together members of the congregation for their mutual benefit'. He was a very active Chairman of the John Evelyn Society and gave several notable slide lectures. One about his predecessors as Vicars of Wimbledon led to a list of the Rectors and Vicars (drawn up by A.W. Hughes Clarke) being placed under a window in the south aisle of St Mary's.

Perhaps Monroe's most enduring achievement was to set up a Parochial

---

A NAVAL ENSIGN IN ST MARY'S

At the top of the nave hangs a white ensign flown by HMS *Inflexible*, one of Admiral Beatty's battle-cruisers, which fought at Jutland in May 1916. Until recently no-one knew how the flag came to be in St Mary's. But in 1986 an old parishioner writing in the magazine claimed that it had been given by Canon Monroe's brother who had served on the *Inflexible* at Jutland. He was promptly corrected by another correspondent who said the brother had not served in the battle at all, but had been at Sheerness in 1920 when the ship had been paid off and probably had then been given the ensign.

Church Council as required by a law of 1919. Previous Vicars had looked for advice to the Churchwardens and to the Vestry. Since the 1880s, however, the Vestry seems to have done little more than appoint the officials and sanction any expenditure or changes in the church; it was also open to any rate-payer, whether a member of the church or not. Monroe wanted elected representatives from each of the five churches in the parish to discuss problems with him and the Churchwardens. Above all, he wanted a finance committee set up 'to relieve the Vicar of the burden of looking after the finances' (which it did so well that it was able to raise the clergy stipend).

Even with such help, the Vicar's work was still unending. One of his successors described the physical strain of being responsible for such a large parish as 'gigantic. You are never free in the evenings and are working from early morning to late evening'. The tasks would have been impossible without the help of some

George Berry, the Parish Clerk from 1892 to 1935.

Curates of 'conspicuous ability', as well as of St Mary's first Deaconess, Ellen Chown, who came in 1914 and did not retire until 1934 when she was 'over eighty'. Along with them worked Churchwardens like John Ferrier from Canon Bell's time who died in 1917 after sixteen year's service (now commemorated by a window in the church) and A.W. Siggers, described as 'the supporter and friend of four Vicars', who resigned in 1932 after eighteen years in office

The longest serving of all the officers, however, was the Parish Clerk, George Berry. Over the centuries St Mary's has had Clerks who served for long periods. Before Haygarth's time they had led the congregation in answering prayers and singing psalms from a reading desk under the pulpit. Now they dealt with parish correspondence and gave the Vicar notice of all baptisms, funerals or special services. George Berry, a builder who took over in 1892, carried out all his duties 'with integrity, faithfulness and wonderful thoroughness'. According to his daughter, Mrs Morrell, 'he loved the work and would have lived at the church if he had had the chance'. Over forty-four years he served five Vicars and when he died in 1935 still in office he was described by the then Vicar as 'a dear friend whose experience and knowledge were of great value'.

That Vicar was Canon Arthur Phelips. He had come to Wimbledon in 1932, as Monroe's immediate successor, the Revd Edward Tupper, had died after little more than a year at St Mary's. Phelips has been described by one of his Churchwardens as 'a good parish priest, charming, kindly and benevolent'. One of his parishioners remembered him tending the roses in the Vicarage garden, pausing to talk to a robin perched on a wheelbarrow. He was good at visiting parishioners. Above all, he was a man who put a firm trust in the Lord, as he showed during his last six years at St Mary's, the period of the Second World War.

The Impact of War
The two world wars imposed great strains on both the Vicar and his parishioners. In the First World War Canon Bell was deeply affected by the deaths of two of his sons in action during the German spring offensive of 1918 and decided to retire in the last months before victory. In the Second, Canon Phelips was clearly upset by the damage to the east window of the church from a V-1 exploding on Wimbledon Park golf course in the summer of 1944 and retired early the next year. Yet both had done their best to sustain the morale of the congregation during some very difficult years.

Both stressed the need for prayer. Bell held 'days of prayer and intercession

An air photograph taken about 1920. It shows St Mary's in the centre, surrounded by the churchyard with its latest extension containing few graves as yet. Below the churchyard is the Old Rectory.

CHURCHYARD		
Pre-1066	Original small 'Burial Ground'	
1776	First extension	to the west 'by the road leading to the churchyard'
1822	Second extension	to the north-west beyond the De Visme tomb
1862	Third extension	to the north, over land once part of the Rectory
1872	Gap Road cemetery laid out	
1920	Fourth extension	to the north of the entrance gates

on behalf of our country and our allies' in August 1914, again early in 1915 and in August 1917 during the terrible Third Battle of Ypres. He was pleased at the great increase in the numbers receiving communion and felt it showed that 'many were turning to God in penitence and faith'. In July 1940 as the Battle of Britain was about to start, Phelips called on his parishioners to be 'earnest and regular' in their prayers. Their response was 'amazing' especially on the National Days of Prayer every September throughout the war.

The terrible reality of war was brought home to the parish in different ways in the two wars. Throughout the First it was the ever-growing list of husbands or sons killed or wounded in action that had the greatest effect. Otherwise, the services were unchanged except for Evensong which 'for the war' started at 6.30 pm instead of 7. A Parochial Working Party was set up to make flannel shirts for soldiers and sailors, and on Harvest Thanksgiving Sunday in October 1915 a special Egg Service was held at which children brought over sixty dozen eggs for wounded soldiers. But perhaps the most notable event at St Mary's throughout

the war was a sermon preached by the Vicar in the autumn of 1917 warning of the danger of taking reprisals on the enemy for their U-boat campaigns and air raids. Most unusually he allowed it to be printed in the parish magazine because of the need to give a clear lead 'at a time when we are tempted to allow our feelings to obscure our judgements'. His attitude to war clearly had an effect on his son, the Bishop of Chichester, in his stand against mass bombing twenty-five years later.

The Second World War was far more drastic in its effects on St Mary's. The blackout forced immediate changes in the times of services: Communion at 9 am instead of 8 in December and January, Evensong at 3 or 3.30 pm instead of 6.30 during the winter.

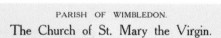

PARISH OF WIMBLEDON.

The Church of St. Mary the Virgin.

WILLIAM WILBERFORCE OF LAURISTON HOUSE WIMBLEDON
Liberator of the Slave. 1759–1833.

Unveiling and Dedication of

The William Wilberforce Memorial

by

The Right Honourable The Lord Mayor of London

and

The Very Reverend The Dean of Worcester.

DECEMBER 17th, 1926.

The cover of the order of service at the dedication of the brass plaque, put up in 1926 on the screen in the chancel as a memorial to William Wilberforce.

Moreover, Christmas midnight services had to be abandoned, while in 1940 the Harvest Thanksgiving was held a fortnight early. Fear of air attack led to pails and stirrup pumps being placed in several parts of the church. In the summer of 1940 with the threat of attack growing ever more likely, it was announced that a firm at Oaklawn in Arthur Road was willing to allow the congregation to use their three 'excellent shelters' on Sundays (though there is no record that they were ever used). Once the Battle of Britain and then the Blitz started, however, the Vicar and his Curates, wearing special ARP armlets with a cross, were constantly on duty, going to every 'incident', comforting the bewildered and helping the dying. Fortunately, the church was never hit during the Blitz, but two fire-watchers were on duty every night, camping out in the vestry, while in the churchyard the graves lost their iron railings 'in compliance with the government's wishes'.

As during the First World War, many people responded to danger by turning to God for help. At Easter 1940 the services were said to have 'seldom been better attended'. By 1941 the number of Easter communions was declared 'satisfactory

The Victorian font inside the baptistery which was built in 1939, with the Old Rectory visible through the window. (*right*) The font cover, given in memory of 2nd Lieutenant Arthur Dowding of the Royal Tank Regiment, killed in France in 1940.

considering the large number of people who have left the parish', while attendances at Christmas services in both 1942 and 1943 showed big increases. There was even time in 1943 to celebrate the centenary of the rebuilding of St Mary's. A special service was held at 5.15 pm on Saturday 20 March in the presence of the Bishop of Southwark; the preacher was the former Archbishop of Canterbury, Lord Lang. A small brochure, *The Heritage of a Thousand Years. St Mary's, the Parish Church of Wimbledon, 1843-1943*, was also produced.

The centenary was described as 'the outstanding event of the year'. In hindsight the most important event of the year was the first stirrings of ecumenism in Wimbledon. The First World War had led to much friendlier relations with the Free Churches. In August 1918 a joint service was held on the Common. The following year there were United Days of Thanksgiving and Prayer for God's guidance during the peace negotiations, and a Christian Social Council was set up to try and improve the lives of the poor. The dramatic events of 1940 began the lowering of the even more entrenched barriers preventing friendly relations with the Roman Catholics. In September 1942 a joint Anglican, Free Church and Roman Catholic meeting was held in Wimbledon Theatre to discuss 'the betterment of social life on Christian principles'. The following year a campaign 'to bring Christian principles to bear in the reconstruction of the modern world' was launched with special preachers in local churches and meetings which attracted 'large audiences'.

In October 1944 came the first sign at St Mary's of coming victory – a 'dim-out' which allowed a small number of lights to be used at services. The following May came VE Day. 'On that evening, in spite of comparatively short notice and hasty preparation, the church was thronged,' the *Parish Magazine* recorded, 'with deeply moved and sincerely thankful people.'

	FURNISHINGS: MEMORIALS TO	
1897	Lectern	Henry Charles Forde
1912	Pulpit and Priest's Desks	John and August Boustead
1920	Screen, South wall of chancel	Llewellyn Longstaff
1925	Brass on Screen	Archbishop Walter Reynolds
1926		William Wilberforce
1935	Tester above Altar	Canon and Mrs Monroe
1949	Cover of Font	2nd Lieut Arthur Dowding

STAINED GLASS WINDOWS

15th Century	Cecil Chapel	Figure of St George
1620s		Cecil Arms
1918	North Aisle	Risen Christ with Angels
1920	South Aisle	Faith, Hope and Charity
1923		St Luke with Angels
1924		Presentation of Infant Jesus
1934	North Aisle	Raymond de Puy, St Francis, St George
1951	Chancel	Christ in glory; below, Virgin and four Evangelists
	(East Window)	Replaced window of 1864, destroyed in 1944

A collection of photographs kept in the Clergy Vestry of the ten Vicars of Wimbledon since 1846. From left to right: (*above*) Adams; Haygarth; Bell; Monroe; Tupper. (*below*) Phelips; Hook; Wright; Clifford Smith; Marshall.

ST MARY'S SINCE 1945

The Post-War Vicars of Wimbledon

'To treat of current events is like walking on ashes beneath which the embers are still glowing,' wrote the Roman poet, Horace, two thousand years ago. His remark could certainly apply to a modern historian dealing with the church since the Second World War and in danger of stirring recent embers into flame. Thanks, however, to the existence of a parish magazine, developments at St Mary's can now be seen in some perspective.

The parish has had a magazine for nearly a hundred years. The first issue probably appeared in 1894 under Canon Haygarth, but the earliest surviving copy dates from January 1915. It was then called *The Wimbledon Parish Magazine*, cost two pence and was bound in with a thirty page Church periodical, *The Sign*, which included articles on Westminster Abbey and Advice to Parents. Since then it has had many titles, while its format, price and style of production have often changed, particularly in the last twenty years. But its value as a source of information on events at the church is unrivalled.

The magazine is especially useful for the insight it gives into the aims, the problems and the reflections on the parish of its last Vicars, three of whom wrote regular articles. In the forty-two years after the end of the war (1945 - 87), as in the previous forty-two, St Mary's had four Vicars:

    1945-53   Canon Norman Hook, MA
    1953-61   Canon Leslie Wright, OBE
    1961-73   Canon Clifford Smith, MA
    1973-87   The Revd Hugh Marshall, MA (from 1978 first Team Rector).

They had to face many serious problems in the post-war world. At home there were 'the years of austerity' in the late 1940s, followed by the 'never had it so good' era under Harold Macmillan, the Labour 'winter of discontent' in the late 1970s, leading to the rise of 'Thatcherism'. Abroad the fears roused by the Cold War and the end of Empire led to Britain joining the Common Market in 1973. In the church there was a religious revival in the 1950s associated with Billy Graham's Greater London Crusade. In the 1960s the Vatican Council produced a dramatic growth in ecumenism, while the publication of John Robinson's *Honest to God* signalled the emergence of a more 'liberal' approach to religion. Then during the 1970s there was a sharp fall in church attendance. Yet conferences, like those at Lambeth, showed that the Anglican Communion was now a world-wide federation of churches.

With all these developments still in the future, Norman Hook's reaction to his appointment as Vicar in 1945 was to tell his new parishioners: 'I am not a party churchman. I should like my ideal church to be a real fellowship.' He added that his other chief aim was 'to strengthen the spiritual life of the church'. In both aims he achieved some considerable success. His impact on the congregation was 'immediate and memorable'. An essentially humble and warm-hearted man, 'he inspired admiration and deep affection'. His sermons were lengthy, but always worth listening to 'for their erudition and lucidity'. He was very good with children and loved taking their Sunday afternoon service. He himself declared that 'being a parson, on the whole, is an exciting business, strenuous, though very happy'. His eight years at St Mary's are notable, above all, for the introduction of the Family Communion Service at 9.30 on Sundays and of study groups known as 'Cells', whose members deepened their faith by discussing the books of the Bible or a modern religious work (his 'most interesting and challenging legacy', according to his successor). He also bought a new Vicarage in Arthur Road and left parish finances in a healthy state.

On Hook's promotion to the Deanery of Norwich in 1953, Leslie Wright became Vicar. Unlike his predecessors over the previous three centuries, he had not been to university. Instead he had joined the army, resigned to enter the Church and had risen to become Chaplain-in-Chief in the RAF. A very kind and genial man, he was noted for his rosy complexion and for wearing a red cassock, a legacy of his time as a Royal Chaplain. Unlike Hook, he was neither an innovator, nor a noted preacher. But he was a good administrator and tireless visitor who wore himself out in the service of his parish. After his death in 1972 a friend commented that 'in his secret life he had the mortification of a saint'. So it is hardly surprising that the development he found 'most encouraging' was the start of prayer groups at St Mary's. He regarded them as 'one of the most effective ways in which we can set forward the Kingdom of God'.

Wright resigned in 1961 as he felt the parish needed a younger man – and presented the church with a silver chalice 'in thanksgiving for the privilege of serving Wimbledon'. His successor, Clifford Smith, had also been a Chaplain to the Forces, but in almost every other way was a very different character. An Oxford graduate and a journalist before entering the Church, he was an excellent preacher who once gave a Lenten course with each sermon based on the title

The east end of the church with the medieval chancel on the right, the Cecil Chapel in the centre, the Clergy Vestry on the left and eighteenth-century tombstones in the foreground.

of a different newspaper. He shared the current enthusiasm for ecumenism, holding frequent meetings with local Roman Catholics and Nonconformists, and helping to draw up a joint statement on Church Unity. When he resigned in 1973

ANN WEDGWOOD AND GEORGE SHRIVE

In a church like St Mary's a great deal depends on the character and leadership of the Vicar – or now the Rector. But, as Leslie Wright acknowledged, the parson's life 'would be intolerable' without lay help. He was referring to the Church-wardens 'who share the work of the parish with me'. But he could equally have included the many men and women who have made up the Parish and Church Committees or who have served St Mary's in innumerable other ways. It is invidious to single out anyone still living, but ideal examples can be found in two outstanding individuals who died within a few months of each other twenty years ago.

Ann Wedgwood (1888-1972) was said to have had 'a profound Christian faith which permanently influenced so many lives in Wimbledon'. For many years she taught at Wimbledon High School. On retiring soon after the end of the war, she became one of Norman Hook's chief advisers on church affairs. She ran the Sunday School during Family Communion; she started Prayer Groups; she organised the first Cells or Study Groups; she even financed a Parish Library and Family Centre at St Mark's Church. In the kindest possible way, 'she stirred the clergy into action'.

George Shrive (1887-1973) also had a profound influence 'on the personal life and worship of Wimbledon'. He too was a schoolteacher, the Headmaster of several local schools, a JP and the first Freeman of the Borough of Merton. At St Mary's he sang in the Choir for many years; after he became blind he sang the hymns from memory. He also organised innumerable fetes and was Secretary to Frank Gentle's Committee charged by Norman Hook to raise £20,000 for the diocese immediately after the war. The money was raised in two years, thanks to George Shrive sending out six thousand letters to possible donors. No wonder that shortly after his death in 1973 a plaque in his memory was placed on the north wall of the chancel.

---

to become Vicar of Broadway, he described the parish as 'wonderful, but complex' and 'well equipped with lay leadership'.

Some of these lay leaders found Clifford Smith a little too easy going. They responded better to his more dynamic successor, Hugh Marshall. At forty the youngest Wimbledon Vicar since Haygarth, Marshall exuded energy, enthusiasm and ideas. He inspired many of the parishioners to work for the church rather than simply give money. He also persuaded the parish to support schemes for helping the unemployed and gaining closer contact with the problems of South Africa by supporting Theo Naledi, a priest from Botswana, while he was studying at London University. (He has since become Bishop of Matabeleland.) But Marshall's greatest achievements were clearly his success in finally building a parish hall, Fellowship House, and in the setting-up in 1978 of a Team Ministry. After over four hundred years of almost second-class status first as a Perpetual Curate and then from 1868 as Vicar, the minister at St Mary's became a Team Rector, with two Vicars of incumbent status who share with him the care of the whole Wimbledon parish of four churches (Christ Church had been made a separate parish in 1961).

Parish Communion and the ASB

With services conducted by four such different, yet dedicated priests, congregations at St Mary's do not seem to have declined as they did in so many parish churches, especially in the 1970s and '80s. Naturally the clergy were still not satisfied. Norman Hook declared that 'the church should be full with every seat occupied every Sunday'. Leslie Wright felt that as the numbers at services were 'tragically out of proportion to those who could be with us', the church was having 'relatively small impact on the community at large'. And they were urged on by a letter to Norman Hook from a parishioner who complained that the services were 'deadly dull', conducted by 'lugubrious-looking' clergy and attended by an equally 'lugubrious-looking' congregation.

First they made sure that St Mary's was a church of which its parishioners could be proud. Norman Hook had the dirty interior lime-washed and a new

Fellowship House.

east window put in to replace the one destroyed in 1944. Four eighteenth-century candelabras were hung over the chancel and the steeple given new oak shingles. But he could not secure approval for a rood screen, which the architect J.S. Comper advised because 'the interior looks unfinished without it'. Then in 1953 Leslie Wright was delighted to see the shields (with coats of arms of local churches, dioceses and lords of the manor connected with Wimbledon) placed on the front of the gallery 'as a visible reminder of all that has been accomplished from the parish church in the past centuries'. But he too found little support for his proposal that the Warrior and Cecil Chapels should be merged, the Cecil tomb removed and the altar placed at the East end for use at weekday Communions. In 1964 Clifford Smith revived the Patronal Festival of the church 'after many years', according to the parish magazine, in fact for the first time since the Reformation. The Sunday nearest to the feast of the Visitation (2 July) was chosen until 1981 when it was altered to 8 September (the Virgin's Nativity). Under Hugh Marshall the bells were recast and rehung in 1984, while 'the most uncomfortable pews in the whole of Christendom' were made more bearable by the 'loving, painstaking work' of Mary Loveband, Norah Humphreys, Gwen Lethbridge and their many helpers in producing 350 beautiful kneelers.

St Mary's was now an ideal setting for more colourful services. The first was suggested by Norman Hook in the parish magazine of July 1948: to play a part in the 'parish communion movement' which was then sweeping across the Church of England by holding 'a communion of the whole congregation every

(*opposite*) The nave seen from the chancel. On the front of the gallery are the shields of dioceses and lords of the manor connected with Wimbledon. Above is the massive Victorian organ. (*right*) One of the 350 kneelers made in the 1980s for the pews in the church. This ecumenical kneeler commemorates the visit to England in 1982 of John Paul II (who stayed on Parkside). It shows the Papal arms and the Pope's signature.

THE ST MARY'S ORGAN

The first organ used in the church since the Reformation was bought in 1810 for one hundred and fifteen guineas. It must have been relatively small, as in 1841 when Gilbert Scott started rebuilding the nave it was removed and reerected in the barn near the Dog and Fox at a cost of five pounds. Only two years later it was sold for twenty-six pounds.

Appropriately the new church was given a new organ. Built by Walker, it was considered 'one of the finest organs in South-Eastern England'. After only thirty-three years' use, however, it had to be completely rebuilt as it had been 'ruined by damp'. By 1926 it needed a further rebuilding. Still blown by hand, it was 'generally acknowledged to be the worst to play for many miles around'. An electric motor was installed and the organ given a new lease of life.

No records seems to have been kept of those who played it during services. But from Vestry Minutes and Parish Magazines, a list can be made of some of the chief organists:

1815-43	John Kelly	1910s	Percy Rideout
1843-54	John Adams	1920s	Percy Moore
1854-69	Keziah Peache	1937-59	Robert Rivers
1869-c1900	William Hope	1959-	Denis Aldersea

The organ.

Sunday'. Nothing happened until Whitsun 1951 when rather hesitantly he started a Family Service at 9.30, especially for parents with young children who 'find it difficult' to come to Holy Communion at 8 or Mattins at 11. He stressed that he did not want anyone 'to transfer their allegiance from Mattins'. Within a year the service had become very popular drawing congregations of about 150, most of them young who enjoyed singing hymns. By 1960 the numbers had grown further and it was proving difficult to keep the service to its promised limit of sixty-five minutes. Since then the 9.30 Sung Eucharist has become the chief service rather than Mattins, with a large number of young families attending every Sunday. For children under three a creche is provided; for those older there is Sunday School, but all come into the church for the last five minutes of the service to receive a blessing.

More experimental services started under Clifford Smith in 1967. As in many other churches, the congregation at Evensong was asked to make responses to new prayers, sing new hymns like 'The Lord of the Dance' and even discuss the sermon. New Communion Services, especially Series 3, used modern English and addressed God as 'you' rather than the traditional 'thou'. Thanks to careful preparation, the new services seem to have been 'generally received with enthusiasm' – but many parishioners preferred the traditional ways. To meet their objections the 1662 Prayer Book was used at the eight o'clock Communion on the second and fourth Sundays of the month as well as for Mattins and Evensong. Otherwise the Alternative Service Book (ASB) came into use from 1980, especially at the 9.30 Sung Eucharist. By the 1980s no parishioner could claim that the services were 'deadly dull'.

The Vicarage, the Field and the Hall
By the 1980s too the surroundings of the parish church had been transformed. Norman Hook earned the gratitude of his successors by buying Newholme, Arthur Road, in 1948 with money given by an anonymous parishioner. It was to be a temporary Vicarage until 'we can build a new permanent one on the acre belonging to the Ecclesiastical Commissioners and reserved for that purpose'. In the intervening years a more permanent house has not been built. Nonetheless, Haygarth's old Vicarage, too large, without electric light and expensive to maintain, was got rid of.

Hook's successor, Leslie Wright, was responsible for buying St Mary's Field in 1956. It cost the church a mere £250, but was accompanied by very restrictive

TWO OF THE EIGHT BELLS WHICH HANG IN THIS TOWER
DATE FROM THE REIGNS OF
KING HENRY VIII AND QUEEN ELIZABETH
A THIRD WAS ADDED IN THE YEAR OF THE CORONATION OF
KING GEORGE I
THE NUMBER WAS INCREASED TO SIX IN THE TIME OF
QUEEN VICTORIA
THE LAST TWO WERE GIVEN IN MEMORY OF
FREDERICK AND ALICE GREEN
IN THE SEVENTEENTH YEAR OF THE REIGN OF
KING GEORGE V

WILLIAM THOMAS | CHURCHWARDENS   HORACE MONROE
ALFRED SIGGERS | VICAR.

IN THE REIGN OF QUEEN ELIZABETH THE SECOND,
THE BELLS OF THIS TOWER WERE RE-CAST AND RE-HUNG
BY WHITECHAPEL BELL FOUNDRY

THE TWO OLDEST BELLS WERE HUNG AS
TOLLING BELL AND CLOCK BELL

A NEW PEAL OF EIGHT WAS CAST USING
METAL FROM SIX OF THE OLD BELLS

THE TENOR WEIGHS 11CWTS
THE TREBLE WEIGHS 3CWT. 1.1B.
AD. 1984·

(*above*) Two tablets in the west porch, commemorating
important moments in the history of the church bells:
the hanging of two new bells in 1927 and the recasting
and rehanging of all the bells in 1984. (*right*) Two of St
Mary's bells, back in the tower after recasting in 1984.

THE CHURCH BELLS

In his short history Jack Harvey described the bells as 'one of the loveliest possessions of St Mary's'. In the medieval church there were 'three belles in the steeple' – until Edward VI's government confiscated them in 1552. One (made about 1520 with the inscription 'Sancte Bartholomee') must soon have been restored and to it was added a second in 1572 (with the inscription 'Praise ye the Lord') and a third in 1715. These three were rehung in the Georgian steeple and then in the Victorian tower. Between 1867 and 1876, they were joined by three more. Fifty years later in 1927, at a time when they were said to be 'dangerous to ring', two further bells were given in memory of Mr and Mrs Green.

In 1984 these eight bells were given a 'major refit'. No work had been done on them for many years and they needed new frames and fittings. The two oldest were simply tuned and rehung. The one from 1520 was fitted with a hammer to strike the hours, while the other from 1572 was given a tolling mechanism. The other six were recast with extra metal at Whitechapel Bell Foundry (where they had all originated) and a new peal of eight bells produced – all with names: Mary, Charles, Mark, Matthew, Luke, Peter, Paul and John. They were rededicated at Evensong on 9 September. The St Mary's Bell Ringers were said 'to be delighted with their tone'.

---

covenants to ensure it was kept as an open space. Not until Clifford Smith's time was a major use found for it – as a car park during the Wimbledon Tennis Fortnight. In 1969 'the first experiment' (with a charge of five shillings a day for a car) raised £121 and was declared 'a great success'. From 1975, a cake, snack or picnic stall was added to the car park and proved equally successful. Thanks to the hard work of many volunteers, the takings rose to over £2,000 in 1978, £8,600 in 1985 and £16,000 in 1992. The money was shared between St Mary's, the diocese and good causes at home and abroad (such as a Youth Club in Battersea and the diocese of Botswana in 1985). But it was stressed that the main aim was not to make money, but 'to give a warm welcome to all visitors to the Wimbledon tennis'. Hence an offer of £40,000 made in 1984 for the right to use the Field for a 'Hospitality Tent' was refused , but only after much debate.

Hugh Marshall was responsible for getting Fellowship House built. The idea of having a parish hall near the church originated in Leslie Wright's time. St Mary's had long owned and used a hall above a furniture shop at the junction of Lancaster Road and the High Street. But it was a quarter of a mile from the church and so could not easily be used after services. A hall by the church would, it was argued, 'help the congregation develop family unity' and might also 'serve the wider community'. So plans were drawn up, provisional planning permission secured, the old hall sold and the money (along with a large sum raised by the congregation) set aside for a new building. Then for over ten years under Clifford Smith nothing seemed to happen, except interminable legal wrangles. As soon as Hugh Marshall arrived in 1974, the troubles were solved, the plans were approved and building started. In just over six months the hall was ready for opening. Its name, Fellowship House, was not liked by everyone, but no better alternative was suggested. Its aim, according to the Vicar, was to be 'a humming centre of study, a place where we can offer help and instruction, and a place where the family of God can meet and grow'.

In the years since its opening, these aims have been abundantly fulfilled. In 1977 a Study Centre was started with courses on prayer, faith and marriage preparation, and others the following year on the Bible, Christian Mysticism and Christian Art and Architecture. They have been well supported. In 1987 a new parish office was added to the hall and a Parish Secretary and Administrative Officer appointed. In addition, innumerable meetings and social events have taken place, making Fellowship House one of the most significant developments in the post-war history of St Mary's.

The Christmas Crib at St Mary's.

CONCLUSION

St Mary's Today

A vibrant and happy community'
This description of the parishioners at St Mary's (since 1988 under the leadership of their second Team Rector, Canon Gerald Parrott) was made recently by 'an observer'. It is shown in the many activities that continue during the week at the church – weekday services, prayer group, bell-ringing, flower arranging, church cleaning – and at Fellowship House – meetings, courses, mother and toddler groups, charity fund-raising events. It is especially evident in the group from King's College School and the parish led by the Revd Robin Stevens, Chaplain at KCS, who every Monday take food, survival bags and warm clothing to the homeless at Waterloo. In early 1991 during a cold spell they even gave temporary shelter to twenty-three homeless men and women in Fellowship House.

Such action is possible because of the 'strong spiritual life' in the parish, noted by Clifford Smith in the early 1970s. It shows in the encouraging attendance at services, above all the 9.30 Sung Eucharist, and the fact that over two hundred go to Communion every Sunday. It shows in the increasing number of baptisms and in the attendance at Sunday School when young children fill Fellowship House. It also shows in the support for Christian Aid, in the existence of House

Canon Gerald Parrott,
Team Rector since
1988.

The Revd Andrew Studdert-Kennedy (second from right) after his first service at St Mary's in July 1989, with Canon Parrott and Joan Ellis, a Lay Reader.

Study Groups, in the close links with Bishop Gilpin's School and in the admirable collection of *Personal Prayers*, 'used and recommended' by parishioners, edited by the present Rector and published in 1991.

In addition, as a fine building the church draws people to worship. After a recent 'face-lift' when the chancel was sealed off for three months while the roof was replaced (and masses of pigeon droppings removed), its return to full use was greeted by a poem in the parish magazine which described it as 'this little rural church set in a town'. No wonder it is popular outside its normal congregation for baptisms and weddings, while a picture of the spire is often used at the start or finish of television transmissions during the tennis fortnight.

The Challenge of the Future

Inevitably the Church faces 'an unpredictable future', as Canon Parrott made clear shortly after his appointment. One major problem common to all churches in England is the shortage of clergy. In the past the parish has been served by many young Curates. At the start of this century (as shown in a photo on page 91) Canon Bell had nine to help him minister to five churches. In the early 1990s St Mary's has been fortunate to be assigned one, Andrew Studdert-Kennedy, for four years' training. The whole parish is now only entitled to three priests of 'incumbent status', the Rector and the two Team Vicars, to serve four churches – St Mary's, St Mark's, St John's and St Matthew's. As a result the clergy are going to be more fully stretched than ever before.

A second problem highlighted by Canon Parrott concerned 'the thousand people who come [to church] at Christmas and not even occasionally on the other normal Sundays'. Along with them are the parents of children at Bishop Gilpin's School and many others who have some link with the Church. Here, he felt, was 'an exciting potential for growth' through further development of the 9.30 Sung Eucharist. The aim of this service 'surely should be to strive to achieve as near perfect a balance as we can between serving the existing congregation and, without diminishing the quality of the worship, to slant its ordering always with half an eye on those we would hope to draw.' And he concluded: 'They will be drawn if they are touched by what ought to be radiating out – the Spirit of God – through the worship of Him, by His people, in His house'.

Celebrating an Anniversary

Faced by such a challenge, it is surely right to remember the achievements of the past and celebrate the 150th anniversary of the reconsecration of St Mary's. Twenty years ago in the parish magazine there had been an appeal 'for some historian to take in hand the history of the ministry at the church and the development of the church building'. This task has at last been accomplished by the present history and by the Church Recording Group. Since 1988 the Wimbledon branch of NADFAS (National Association of Decorative and Fine Arts Societies) has been making an inventory of everything of value in St Mary's – its memorials, plate, windows, stonework, wood and other features – along with notes on their makers, their donors and where possible their history. So everything known about the church is now recorded in a way it never has been before.

Certain things, however, cannot be recorded. A church is not just a building; it is the House of God. So over many centuries the people of Wimbledon have come to St Mary's Sunday after Sunday to offer praise and worship, and to receive help and grace. They have had the great events of life – baptisms, marriages, funerals – blessed there. Such visits are largely unrecorded, as are their effects. There can, however, be no doubt that the church dedicated by Archbishop Howley on 20 March 1843 'to Almighty God and the celebration of divine worship according to the rites and ceremonies of the Church of England' is certainly fulfilling its purpose.

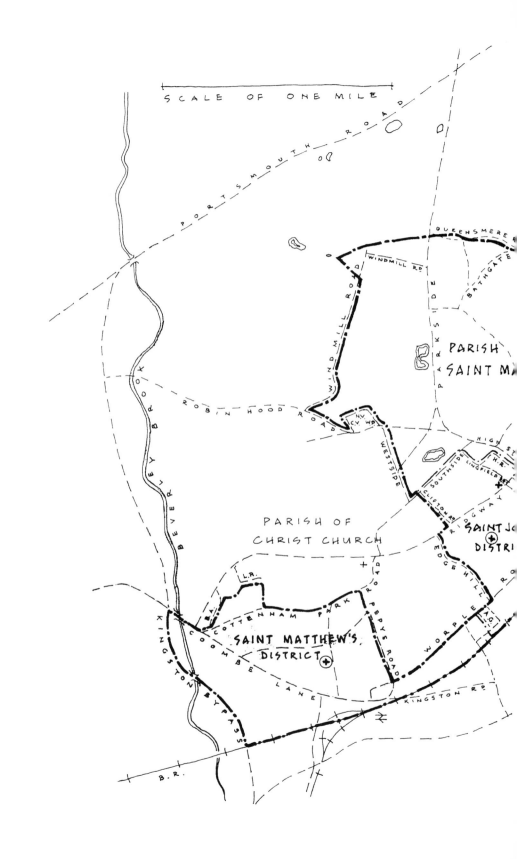

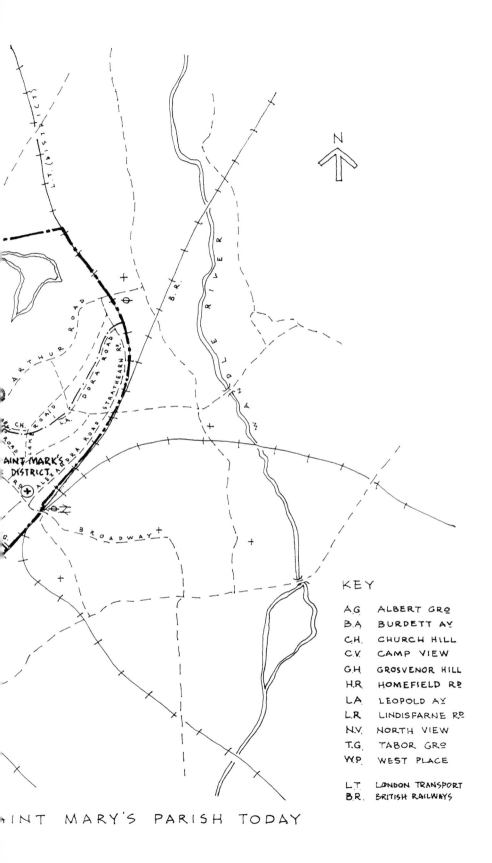

N

KEY

A.G. ALBERT GRO
B.A. BURDETT AV
C.H. CHURCH HILL
C.V. CAMP VIEW
G.H. GROSVENOR HILL
H.R. HOMEFIELD RD
L.A. LEOPOLD AV
L.R. LINDISFARNE RD
N.V. NORTH VIEW
T.G. TABOR GRO
W.P. WEST PLACE

L.T. LONDON TRANSPORT
B.R. BRITISH RAILWAYS

SAINT MARY'S PARISH TODAY

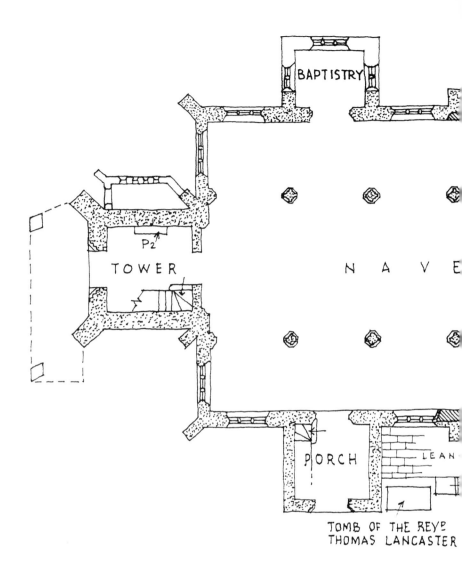

BAPTISTRY

P₂

TOWER   N A V E

PORCH   LEAN

TOMB OF THE REVᴰ
THOMAS LANCASTER

0   5   10   20   30   40   50
SCALE   OF   FEET

REDRAWN FROM A PLAN BY THOS. G. JACKSON

SAINT MARY'S CHURCH

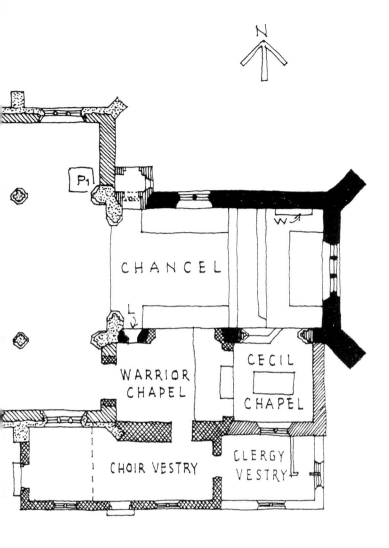

N

CHANCEL

P₁

W↗

CECIL CHAPEL

WARRIOR CHAPEL

CHOIR VESTRY

CLERGY VESTRY

KEY

▓ 15TH CENTURY ON OLDER FOUNDATIONS
▨ 1626 ~ 1630
▧ 1786
▒ 1843
▥ 1860
▦ 1920
☐ MODERN

L = LYCHNOSCOPE
P₁ = PULPIT
P₂ = PERRY MONUMENT
W = WALTER MONUMENT

WIMBLEDON

Chief Sources

ARCHIVES

British Library: Althorp Papers (Letters of Spencer family); Lansdowne MSS (Papers of
Sir William Cecil)

Lambeth Palace: Visitation Returns for 1758, 1788, 1806, 1858, 1862; Records of the
Consecration, 1843

Public Record Office: Religious census 1851; Wills of Thomas Green and Thomas Mylling

Surrey Record Office: Church Enlargement Papers, 1841-43; Churchwardens' Accounts,
1741-1871; Evidence to Select Committee on Public Worship Bill, 1875; Papers on
Church Fabric, 1905-61; Parish Magazines, 1915-1944; Preacher's Book, 1880-94;
Register of Services, 1910-1939; Vestry Minutes, 1743-1885

St Mary's Vestry: Parish Magazines, 1945-92; Vestry Minutes, 1885-1992

Wimbledon Museum: Vestry Notebook, 1848

Wimbledon Reference Library: Parochial Reports, 1859-1916

ARTICLES

Revd C. Chamberlain: 'Canon Haygarth', *Wimbledon and Merton Annual*, 1905

Sir T. Jackson: 'The Church of St Mary the Virgin, Wimbledon', *Surrey Archaeological
Collections*, Vol 34, 1921

Dr E. Veale: 'The Parish of St Mary's 100 Years Ago', Typescript, Wimbledon Society
Museum

'Inventory of Church Goods, 1552', *Surrey Archaeological Collections*, Vol 4, 1869

BOOKS AND PAMPHLETS

On St Mary's

J. Harvey, *History of the Parish Church of St Mary the Virgin, Wimbledon*, 1972

A. Hughes Clarke, *Monumental Inscriptions in the Church and Churchyard of St Mary's
Wimbledon*, 1934
The Parish Register of Wimbledon, Co. Surrey, 1924

A. Whitehead, *The Bells of St Mary's*, 1986

On Parish Churches

G. Addleshaw and F. Etchells, *The Architectural Setting of Anglican Worship*, 1948

J. Bettey, *Church and Parish*, 1987

F. Bottomley, *The Church Explorer's Guide*, 1978

C. Platt, *The Parish Churches of Medieval England*, 1981

On the Church of England

G. Cuming, *History of the Anglican Liturgy*, 1982

H. Davies, *Worship and Theology in England*, Vols III-V, 1960-65

Revd A. Eaton, *The Faith, History and Practice of the Church of England*, 1957

A. Hastings, *History of English Christianity, 1920-90* (1991)

E. Norman, *Church and Society in England, 1770-1970*, 1976

On the Church in London and Surrey

J. Blair, *Early Medieval Surrey*, 1991

R. Mudie-Smith, *The Religious Life of London*, 1904

D. Robinson, *Pastors, Parishes and People in Surrey*, 1989

On Personalities

Dictionary of National Biography, Lives of Archbishop Howley and Sir George Gilbert Scott, 1900

Sir G. Gilbert Scott, *Personal and Professional Recollections*, 1879

On Wimbledon

P. Fawcett, *Memories of a Wimbledon Childhood, 1906-18*, 1981

R. Milward, *Early Wimbledon*, 1969; *Tudor Wimbledon*, 1972; *Wimbledon in the Time of the Civil War*, 1976; *Georgian Village*, 1986; *Historic Wimbledon*, 1989

Sources Of Illustrations

Front cover: Micky White, by courtesy of the Wimbledon Tennis Museum

Back cover: Wimbledon Society

Dr Thomas Cocke, p 32; Lambeth Palace Library, p 10; Denise Murgatroyd, p 109; NADFAS, pp 29, 114 (below); Canon Parrott, p 91; Raynes Park Camera Club, p 112; Russells, pp 9, 21 (below), 32, 36, 85, 102, 104, 111, 114 (above), 116; St Mary's Parish Office, pp 2, 24, 41, 47, 61 (top right and below), 88, 93, 107, 110; Surrey Record Office, pp 27, 31, 45, 48, 51 (below); A.P. Whitehead, 1, 3, 64; Wimbledon Society, pp 11, 19, 21 (above), 25, 35, 38, 43, 51 (above), 52, 55, 56, 58, 59, 61 (top left), 62, 69, 70, 74, 76, 78, 81, 90, 92, 94, 95, 97, 98, 99, 101; Margaret Young, p 118.

Index